FULLY STAFFED

FULLY
STAFFED
ERIC CHESTER

THE DEFINITIVE GUIDE TO
FINDING & KEEPING
GREAT EMPLOYEES
IN THE WORST LABOR MARKET EVER

Published and distributed by:

SOUND WISDOM
P.O. Box 310
Shippensburg, PA 17257-0310

717-530-2122

info@soundwisdom.com

www.soundwisdom.com

TP: 978-1-64095-180-8

HC: 978-1-64095-112-9

Ebook: 978-1-64095-113-6

Library of Congress Cataloging-in-Publication Data
Names: Chester, Eric, author.
Title: Fully staffed : the definitive guide to finding & keeping great
    employees in the worst labor market ever / Eric Chester.
Description: Shippensburg, PA : Sound Wisdom, [2020] |
Identifiers: LCCN 2019056935 | ISBN 9781640951129 (hardcover) | ISBN
    9781640951136 (ebook)
Subjects: LCSH: Employees--Recruiting. | Employee selection. | Employee
    retention.
Classification: LCC HF5549.5.R44 C44 2020 | DDC 658.3--dc23
LC record available at https://lccn.loc.gov/2019056935

For Worldwide Distribution, Printed in the U.S.A.

2 3 4 5 6 7 8 9 / 30 29 28 27 26 25 24 23

ACKNOWLEDGMENTS

In today's brutal war for labor, it's easier to get an employer to send a customer to their direct competitor than it is to find one who's willing to share a tactic they've hit upon to recruit great employees. That's why my first debt of gratitude goes to the 50+ employers who've "peeled back the curtain" in their business to share their innovative recruiting strategies in this book.

Many thanks to my editors, Carolyn Daughters and Jennifer Janechek, PhD. I can only imagine how difficult it must be to transform the scrambled thoughts and ideas I put onto a page into something that actually makes sense to the reader. Every author should be so lucky.

My buddies who are authors often lament the challenges they have with their publishers. I can only listen in silence, because my publishing team at Sound Wisdom is an author's dream. These people truly love their authors and exist only to help us spread our expertise, our voice, and our vision through the creation of amazing books and materials. Wow. Thank you, SW!

But my biggest debt of gratitude goes to Rae Nelson and Karl Haigler, the brilliant management consulting team of Haigler Enterprises who poured countless hours of research, interviews, and sweat into this project. There's no way this book would have happened without Karl and Rae, and I am truly blessed that they chose to devote their undying passion for workforce development to this project.

CONTENTS

PART I

SURVIVING
THE SHORTAGE

Chapter 1

THE PERFECT STORM
Why You're Struggling to Find Employees

Imagine the headlines in today's paper are exactly as they were back on October 10, 2008. The Dow has plunged to half the value of the day before. There's widespread panic as investors are pulling out of the market at lightning speed. Banks are closing. Stockbrokers and hedge fund managers on Wall Street are considering jumping out of their plush skyscraper offices.

Unless you're operating a grief counseling center, in all likelihood your business's bottom line is going to take a serious hit. You're going to have to make severe cuts on the expense side of the ledger just to keep afloat. It's not going to be pretty.

However, there is a silver lining.

You can take down those "Now Hiring" signs and pull all your "Help Wanted" ads off Craigslist and Indeed. See, you're about to witness a BOOM in the number of job applications flowing through your inbox like you haven't experienced in a decade. Your employee turnover problem will be all but eliminated! In the past, you may have struggled to find a warm-bodied person to take a job among your ranks who has no felonies and can pee in a cup to pass a drug test. Now, you'll probably be turning away MBAs who are willing to drive a truck, flip burgers, sweep floors, and work nights and weekends without any qualms at all!

Hooray! That dreadful hiring curse you've dealt with for what seems like an eternity has just been lifted!

Okay, maybe I'm being a tad overdramatic there, but you get the drift. In a bad economy, the good news is that a surplus of labor competes for jobs.

Unfortunately, the opposite is also true. In a good economy, the bad news is that the labor market tightens and businesses have to compete for workers. Obviously, the higher the skill level, the fiercer the competition. These are the facts, and these facts are crushing you.

Is This Book Right for You?

The current reality is that the labor market is nearly drained. You need many more skilled workers than are available, and you picked up this book because you're having trouble finding and keeping solid workers in your business or organization.

If the above statement isn't true, you should consider reading a different book (and do a happy dance followed by a celebratory toast).

But if you're still reading, then there couldn't be a better, more timely book for you.

When you first got into business, or when you were first promoted into a managerial or supervisory role, you probably thought that your biggest problem would be finding and attracting new customers, clients, patients, etc. Right?

But all those early struggles now pale in comparison to the challenges you're facing. How in the world are you supposed to find and keep employees, especially those in the less desirable positions you rely on so heavily? Let's be honest: these jobs are taken by people who earn less money and make fewer decisions than those to whom they report. In theory, these jobs shouldn't be so hard to fill. And yet, somehow they have been.

Feeling frustrated, exasperated, and perhaps even angry with this new emerging workforce, you want to know if there's a solution to your dilemma. You're dying to know how you can attract a better qualified and more dedicated workforce. There must be a way.

Make no mistake, it isn't just about hiring. You're also searching desperately for a way to stop the mass exodus of your best workers so you can finally reach business nirvana, that mythical place where you're FULLY STAFFED with the right people happily engaged in the right jobs. So you can once again focus on building and improving your business.

Your pain is real. And you're not alone.

If you're suffering, then you're among the vast majority of business owners, leaders, executives, managers, and supervisors in North America—and, for that matter, most countries that operate according to the principles of a free market economy.

In the United States, for example, the unemployment rate is at a 50-year low. Employers of *all sizes* and in *virtually every industry* are struggling mightily to fill positions at *all levels*. And when it comes to filling positions perceived as unsexy, that's where employers' pain is the greatest.

What's a Sexy Job—and What's Not?

What's sexy? What's not? Let me answer those questions with a question.

Q: What do professional dancers, actors, musicians, and athletes have in common?

A: According to the Bureau of Labor Statistics, they're listed as the top dream jobs that our nation's youth aspire to hold one day.

What jobs didn't make this list? Roofer, custodian, waitress, auto mechanic, welder, truck driver, short order cook, pest control technician, retail cashier, call center representative, senior caregiver, sanitation worker, hotel housekeeper, and the ten other positions in your organization that immediately rushed into your mind.

While your life and mine might be less colorful if there were fewer musicians and athletes, imagine life without someone to change the brake pads in your car, patch the potholes in the street you commute on each day, bus the dishes at the table where you've just been seated, unclog the sewer line in your bathroom, and tighten the bolts on the jet you'll board in a few weeks.

Many perceive these jobs as unsexy.

But those aren't the only jobs labeled as such. Jobs as accountants, administrative clerks, production managers, traffic cops, sales reps, and middle school counselors could also be classified as unsexy. In fact, the only conventionally sexy jobs are those where someone is making huge bank doing something many other people would be willing to do for little or no money—and they're getting loads of positive attention and ego-stroking in the process.

Imagine being a talk show host, or a YouTube star, or a professional skateboarder, or a dolphin trainer at Sea World, or a tour manager for a rock star, or an actual rock star. You get the idea.

Fame, fortune, and the ability to call the shots and work *when* we want, *where* we want, and *with whom* we want—who doesn't dream of that? And who among us can honestly admit that they don't at all envy the chosen few who've magically found the Holy Employment Grail?

Reality check: For every job that the masses would define as "sexy," there are 10,000 or 100,000 or 1,000,000 that those same people would quickly dismiss, saying, "No way, no how! I'm glad somebody else will do that job, but it ain't my jam."

Feeling anxious? Are the jobs you're looking to fill among the 1,000,000 that are easily dismissed?

If so, please don't take offense.

It doesn't necessarily mean that the jobs themselves are unsexy.

It doesn't mean that your industry, your company, or your brand is unsexy.

And it doesn't mean that you have to employ people who will produce less-than-sexy results for your organization.

An unsexy job is simply a perception. If you want to change that perception, you must first acknowledge and accept that the negative perception exists. Do that, and you can begin to make the unsexy sexy.

I'm suggesting that you can make any job one that is appealing in the eyes of the candidates you're hoping to attract.

More on that later.

For now, let's get back to understanding why the perfectly honorable open positions at your company—jobs for which you offer a fair compensation, jobs that were good enough for you and for your parents and for their parents—are so doggone hard to fill.

A Perfect Storm

Yes, the labor crisis is real. No one thing has caused the shortage; rather, a combination of factors has led us to this point. To determine the best strategies for overcoming these factors and winning the talent war, we must come to grips with five demographic, economic, technological, educational, and societal factors that have created a perfect hiring and retention storm.

1. The cupboards are bare. Demographers have predicted for quite some time that a labor shortage would come—and they were right. Baby Boomers (born 1946–1963) in the United States are retiring at the rate of more than 10,000 people per day. Their successor, Generation X (born 1964–1979), is a much smaller generation in size, which creates a leadership shortage. The much-maligned generation of Millennials (born 1980–2000) is sizable, but they have entered the workforce with a vastly different idea of what work, career, and the employer/employee relationship should look like.

It's still too early to predict the attitudes and behaviors of Gen Z (born 2001–2012) toward work, but initial signs point to their being even more difficult to engage than their Millennial predecessors. They are also huge in numbers. When combined with the second wave of Millennials, those born after 1990, they comprise nearly a third of our workforce.

Let's forgo the book-length analysis on generational demographics. The real point is this: even though there might appear to be enough potential workers to fill the job openings that currently exist, the percentage of adequately qualified workers who actually want those jobs or will accept those jobs is shrinking. The takeaway? The labor pool is dangerously low.

2. The dollars don't make sense. When more than 200 fast food workers walked off their jobs in New York City back in 2012, they launched the "Fight for $15" war. These restaurant workers sought to unionize and demanded higher wages. In most places, it has worked, and wages are on the rise.

Unfortunately for the millions of employers who've always depended on young, unskilled, hourly workers, this movement has been a punch to the gut. It has also been bad news for teens when employers that have traditionally been their source for first jobs can't justify paying them what the government demands. Employers have slashed hours for their employees and turned to automation to accomplish many tasks once earmarked for teen and entry-level workers.

Rising wages in the restaurant industry have created big problems in all industries. If an unskilled part-time burger flipper in Chicago can command $15 per hour, what's a comparable wage for a muffler installer, a law office receptionist, a community pool lifeguard, and a sewer line rooter technician?

3. Technology is creating as many problems as it's solving. It's to your advantage when you can count on a robot to do the work of one or many. Robots are diligent, and they don't call in sick. They won't cheat you, they won't ask for a raise, and they won't abandon you for another job that's paying 50 cents more per hour down the street. Sweet, sweet music to a business owner's ears.

Unfortunately, machines and robots break. And if they're connected to the Internet, they can be hacked and destroyed from across the planet. Machines like these are expensive to own or rent, and in spite of the investment required they can become obsolete overnight.

Furthermore, solutions to these kinds of challenges require the support of highly trained, well-paid technicians who know how to diagnose, repair, and replace. (Technicians, of course, are in very high demand and short supply.)

Your frontline workforce needs to be techno-savvy, which is the calling card of the young. But your workforce must also know how to implement creative workarounds when the Internet is down and your technology is in a state of disrepair. That's the calling card of the mature, experienced employee.

CASE IN POINT

I recently had a meal prepared at a national burrito chain. It's the kind of restaurant where the worker assembles the meal in front of you as you walk down the assembly line with them.

When I got to the cashier, I asked for a Diet Coke to go with my order.

"The Diet Coke line on our new soft drink dispenser is jammed today, and no one here knows how to unclog it," the cashier told me.

I wanted to sit down and enjoy my customized burrito, but I was now being informed that no sugar-free drinks were available on the premises to wash it down.

"Miss, this restaurant shares a parking lot with a large discount grocery store," I said to the cashier. "In five minutes, for less than $10, you could have five two-liter bottles of Diet Coke on hand to keep customers like me happy. That would probably be enough to get you through the dinner rush. And at the price you charge for a Diet Coke, you'd triple the owner's money before you even opened the second bottle!"

"We have no process for that," she said. "I have no idea how to open this register to get $10 out, and if I could open the register, the cameras would catch me and I'd get fired."

Technology is essential to your success, but if your employees are unwilling or unable to provide an intelligent human interface, they're essentially the human equivalent of a vending machine.

---

4. A degree is your only golden ticket. Another key element of the perfect storm of issues plaguing the labor pool for perceived unsexy jobs is the cultural shift toward higher education. Children are raised from a very young age to believe that a college degree is the one and only way to get ahead in life.

High school graduates have been flocking to universities because they think it's what they have to do to succeed. Many enter college unsure of what career they want to pursue and end up chasing outlandish dreams with low employment potential. What the narrative leaves out is that a job seeker boasting a PhD in Roman History is going to have a much more difficult time finding employment than a certified welder. The PhD also may not earn as much as the welder.

In 2016, 33.4 percent of Americans 25 or older reportedly said they had completed at least a bachelor's degree. Those are the highest numbers ever reported according to the U.S. Census Bureau. That still leaves most potential workers without a four-year college degree, but the number of college graduates seeking and having trouble finding white-collar work based on the degrees they earned is staggering.

Many high-demand jobs that pay well don't require a high school diploma or even a GED. According to the Georgetown Center on Education and the Workforce, more than 30 million jobs in the United States pay an average of $55,000 per year and don't require a bachelor's degree.

The idea that a good job (or any job) will be waiting for every college graduate is a myth. Floods of 20-something grads with newly minted liberal arts degrees are chasing their dreams in broadcasting, film production, and political science and will soon face the reality that the demand for their expertise is nearly nonexistent. They'll take a job as a barista or Uber driver and live in the basement of their parents' home, eagerly awaiting their big break.

You've probably heard this scary statistic: Americans owe more than $1.56 trillion in student loan debt, spread out among about 45 million borrowers. That's about $521 billion more than the total US credit card debt.

Among the class of 2018, 69 percent of college students took out student loans. They graduated with an average debt of $29,800, including both private and federal debt. Meanwhile, 14 percent of their parents took out an average of $35,600 in federal Parent PLUS Loans.

And don't forget the interest compiling on their college loan debt.

As a former high school teacher, coach, and administrator and as an invited speaker to more than 1,500 schools across the United States and Canada, I'm hyperaware of the fact that the realities of today's job market often aren't shared with young people. Parents are busy dreaming about how a college degree is going to ensure their children's future success. Their children, in turn, are busy dreaming about becoming the next big social media influencer or YouTube star.

Non-vocational teachers, counselors, and administrators aren't helping things. Their job is to help students achieve the grades and scores necessary to get into the colleges of their (or their parents') dreams. That's why these school officials don't usually talk to students about how the standardized achievement tests they spent the last three months studying for will have little relevance for them in the future. Kids are left thinking that the only way they can support themselves (and one day a family) and live a great life is if they focus all their energy and passion on getting into and graduating from college instead of mastering a skill or trade.

Think about it. And sigh about it. But don't just throw your hands in the air. Instead, recognize the situation for what it is and do your small part to stop perpetuating the myth.

5. But what will other people think? When I graduated from high school in the 70s, I had three choices:

1. go to college

2. learn a trade

3. join the military

My parents made it abundantly clear that continuing to live with them rent-free wasn't on the menu. They told me it was time to get out there and make something of myself. You know, sink or swim.

Back then, my parents had two televisions, and I got all my news—and most of my entertainment—through the three network channels available. When I was 18, the world seemed like an awfully huge place with a lot of scary stuff going on way over on the other side of the planet.

At the time, I was semi-aware of some of the career opportunities in metro-Denver (the only place I'd ever lived), and I knew what some of my friends were planning to do after graduation.

I didn't play an instrument, and I couldn't sing or dance, so I didn't see a future as a rock star. I had no skill in acting, so I never once considered being a TV or movie star. I was a mediocre high school athlete, so I had no chance of playing sports in college. Becoming a professional athlete in football, baseball, hockey, basketball, golf, or tennis never once entered my mind.

The way I saw it, I wanted a good life, but whatever job, field, or career I chose was my business. My choice had to please only me and my parents (not necessarily in that order).

Who else would ever know what I did for a living? And why would anyone else care?

The world was huge, and my influences were few. Outside of a few young actors, I knew of no one even close to my age who was making big bucks. Success was a long road that began with getting a degree, finding a job at a big company, starting out at the bottom, keeping my nose to the grindstone, and rising through the ranks until I gained enough experience to provide real expertise and value.

Man, I know I sound old. And I guess I am.

My kids and grandkids have grown up in a world where 8-year-olds become instant superstars on *America's Got Talent*. Where 14-year-old gymnasts win Olympic gold and land mega-million-dollar endorsement contracts. Where professional video gamers and sunglass-wearing poker players are considered "athletes," and their "sports" are broadcast on ESPN. Where the 7-year-old YouTube star of *Ryan's Toy Review* earned more than $22 million dollars in 2018 simply unwrapping and playing with new toys. (Boy, there ought to be a law against that kind of brutal child labor!) Where the next social media sensation is just a viral discovery away, prompting teens to rack up friends and followers by the hundreds and thousands.

Is it any wonder why so many 16-year-olds show up for their first jobs with a "you want me to do what kind of grunt work for a measly $10 per hour" attitude?

Separating Effort from Reward

Your emerging workforce has been completely submerged in a culture filled with images, videos, and 24/7 stories showing their peers being paid ridiculous sums of money for what typically amounts to no real contribution to the greater good. Stories of 19-year-olds making an honest living as drywall installers or rental car agents are nowhere to be found.

While the odds of your frontline workers replicating that kind of funny-money success are slim to none (they stand a better chance of winning the lottery), the notion that they are only one viral video or one cool app away from owning a private island is firmly implanted somewhere in their DNA.

I would be shocked if my own adult kids (born in the 80s) and all those who came with and after them didn't at some level believe the hype. It's no wonder that so many young people think there's a shortcut or a "cheat sheet" path to fame, fortune, and a life of luxury.

In my first business book, *Employing Generation Why: Understanding, Managing, and Motivating Your New Workforce*, I claimed that the millions upon millions of post-Generation Xers are intently focused on finding ways to *separate effort from reward*.

I stand by that statement today.

This Storm Isn't Subsiding Anytime Soon

The five factors that have created this labor shortage are very real. Thankfully, understanding the "enemy" is the first step in defeating it.

You can't change demographics, the economy, the education system, technology, or society by yourself. What you can do is embrace what is happening in those arenas and navigate the seas ahead.

That, my friends, is what this book is all about.

I've gone behind the curtain to study hundreds of great companies and interview thousands of owners, managers, and leaders in businesses and industries that aren't considered sexy. This experience has enabled me to uncover the strategies and tactics that are most effective in attracting, recruiting, developing, and, yes, even retaining amazing employees at all levels.

I'm firmly convinced that amid this raging storm it's possible not only to survive this labor shortage but also to THRIVE.

Allow me to take you behind the scenes to show you how great employers are doing just that…

Chapter 2

STOP FISHING
And Start Hunting

In the current hiring climate, it is crucial to be thoughtful and strategic about how you recruit employees. Gone are the times in which you could hang a "Help Wanted" sign on the window of your business and expect talent to come in droves. In today's world, the employer has to do the job *hunting*.

I know from personal experience that dropping a line in the talent pool isn't going to net you the result you want—"bites" from job candidates with the necessary skill set, a strong work ethic, and a commitment to your business.

I've been a researcher, author, and speaker for 30-plus years. My wife, Lori, is a highly successful sales rep for a medical supply company, managing a territory that spans four large states. No married couple in their right minds with that much going on professionally would even consider starting another side business, right?

Well call us crazy, because that's exactly what we did.

Lori and I have long wanted to join forces and start up a business together. But with our busy careers—along with being the patriarch and matriarch of a large blended family that includes five adult children and eight grandchildren—we both felt strongly that any enterprise we chose

to pursue would have to be a low-maintenance, self-service-type business like public storage or a laundromat.

With a father and two brothers who work as auto mechanics, Lori grew up in a car-centered family and believes in the value of keeping her car spotlessly clean. Lori is also a certified veterinarian technician and volunteers at a vet clinic near our home a few days each month. You might say that in our home, there's a passion for clean cars and happy dogs.

A couple years ago, we bought an acre and a half of commercially zoned property that's just a stone's throw away from our home. Our goal? To design, build, and open a modern, first-class car wash. Oh, and we wanted our enterprise to include two private bays where our customers could wash their dogs in a "self-service" dog wash tub with soaps and cleansers specially formulated for their furry friends.

Our plan called for a fully automated, self-service business with the capability to accept cash, coin, and credit card payments. With no human intervention needed to complete transactions, we thought we would have to come down to the wash only every few days to dump a trashcan or two, collect the cash, and make it to the bank before closing.

That's how we drew it out on paper anyway.

We couldn't have been more wrong.

As of this writing, Camelot Car and Dog Wash has been open for a little more than a year, and it's doing very well. Our giant castle-themed structure punctuates the horizon in Golden, Colorado, catching the attention of all passing motorists. And when it comes to equipment and amenities, we didn't cut any corners in our mission to build the finest car wash of its kind on the planet. The reviews clearly show that our customers LOVE taking their cars, trucks, boats, trailers, motorcycles, RVs, and furry friends to "the castle."

Trouble in the Kingdom

Although we're proud of our enterprise, we discovered that when it comes to keeping Camelot fully operational, it is a million miles away from being a self-service establishment. (Yes, we claim sole responsibility for being ignorant as to what all is involved. But that's fodder for another book.)

The fact is, Lori and I were spending an enormous amount of time at the castle doing the very non-sexy work of dumping trash, sweeping concrete, scraping mud off the floor of the bays, and picking up sopping wet dog fur.

But that's just the start. Our operation is highly technical, with millions of dollars of sophisticated equipment housed in an elaborate equipment room resembling NORAD. The equipment room features complex computers, hydroelectric pumps, water heaters and boiler systems, air compressors, a gazillion solenoids and high-pressure hoses and fittings, and complicated-looking gadgets I can't even pronounce, much less repair.

Forget any get-rich-quick, "self-service" pipe dreams and schemes. Lori and I needed help—and we needed it YESTERDAY!

We're a lean startup with a hefty business loan, and our cash flow prevented us from hiring a full-time manager. Thus, we hoped we could find a smart technician who had the work ethic of a Midwest farmer. Someone who lived nearby so they could come at the first sign of trouble. Someone who would be willing to take on this difficult job for the same wages they would earn as a retail cashier or fry cook.

The person we needed would not only have to understand all the various equipment, but also be able to maintain it and even repair it when it broke down. That same person would also need to sweep, mop, plow snow, and clean dog fur off the walls, ceilings, and floors. Oh yeah, and scoop the thick mud that drops off vehicles onto the cement floor before it goes down the drain into the holding tanks, where it would eventually have to be pumped out by a pricey Air-Vac service.

Where Art Thou, Mighty Knight?

I began posting ads all over the Internet and local job boards using such keywords as "carwash attendant," "HVAC mechanic," "repair technician," and even "mud scooper." I spelled out the demands of the job and basic skills necessary, along with the flexible hours and the well-above-minimum starting wage.

After all, even though this was an unusual job requiring a lot of unrelated but essential skills, I felt that for the right person, working at the castle would indeed be a sexy job—one complete with:

- Above-average pay

- Super flexible hours

- No demanding, finger-in-the-face boss on the premises

- Continual growth and development with no two days being the same

- Casual Friday dress code (and at the castle, every day is like Friday)

- Free unlimited car and dog washes (of course!)

"WOW!" I said, patting myself on the back. "What college student or recent retiree wouldn't want *that* kind of a job?"

And so I sat back and waited for the calls, texts, and e-mail applications to pour in.

My "brilliant" online ads brought in zero candidates. Not one. Nada. Zilch. Zippo.

It Was Time to Stop Fishing... and Start Hunting

A few weeks into the process, I came to the realization that I'm an inexperienced fisherman, and I was fishing in uncharted waters. Despite dangling what I thought was attractive bait on the end of my hook, the fish around me simply weren't biting.

Then it dawned on me. No teenager, no college kid, and certainly no retiree in the land was waking up each day thinking, *Gee, if only I could find a job where I could fix water leaks, clean up dog fur, and scoop me some mud!*

Frustrated with the results of my wild fishing expedition, I decided to look at recruiting in an entirely different way.

I grabbed a blank sheet of paper and a pen and started writing down a complete description of the ideal person I needed for the castle. At the top of the page, I wrote, "Seeking a knight who can fix and maintain shiny armor." I then wrote the following thoughts that came into my head:

If I could wave a magic wand, and the perfect employee would suddenly appear, that employee would…

- Live nearby (be able to get to the castle in 5–10 minutes)
- Be able to work 15–20 hours per week, including nights and weekends
- Have practical experience in plumbing, HVAC, and mechanical repair
- Be friendly and courteous—able to interact with customers and make each person and pet feel welcome
- Be computer savvy or at least computer literate
- Be willing to do regular clean-up and maintenance, as well as the dirtiest tasks and chores
- Be a self-starter, proactively watching for minor issues and solving them before they grow into big problems requiring major technical maintenance
- Be coachable and eager to learn
- Be happy for the opportunity to work at this wash
- Last but not least, that person would be a kindhearted soul who I would genuinely like and trust. (After all, a lot of cash comes into the castle.)

Now, I know what you're thinking.

"Yeah, right. We're all looking for that guy or gal. Stand in line, buddy."

But I knew that guy or gal was out there looking for a home.

Then one day I stared at the giant "M" whitewashed on the side of Lookout Mountain rising high above the town of Golden. And it hit me.

Hey! That M stands for "Mines." As in Colorado School of Mines, a very challenging school with incredibly high academic standards. Some of the finest mechanical engineers in the world have graduated from Mines!

In a flash, I dashed off to Mines with a dozen FREE CAR WASH cards and a pocketful of FREE DOG WASH tokens. Inside the mechanical engineering building, I found professors, graduate assistants, and instructional staff. I introduced myself as the owner of that large castle down the street, told them it's actually a state-of-the-art car wash, and said I'd love for them to try it out. I asked if they had a dog. If they did, I gave them a FREE DOG WASH token.

Most of the people I met were kind but in a hurry, yet a few engaged me in conversation. I told them that I wanted to find a student, hopefully one with a few more years of school left. A Golden native who lived nearby. Someone looking for an interesting part-time job with decent pay and hours that could bend around classes and studies. Someone seeking practical, hands-on experience working on sophisticated computer-driven hydroelectric pumps and vacuum systems since the equipment required lots of routine maintenance and repair.

I also made it clear that the "knight" I was searching for had to have an A+ work ethic. (And who knows a student's work ethic better than their teacher or coach, right?)

Two of the instructional staff independently suggested I talk to the same person: Brady Robinson.

I reached out to Brady and invited him to explore some exciting possibilities at the castle.

The Hunt Yielded the Knight
I Was Looking For

Brady has been everything Lori and I could have possibly hoped for and more. He's never missed a day, has kept the castle spotlessly clean, and has saved me many thousands of dollars in costly service calls from the local car wash service company.

Brady is absolutely awesome with my customers. He knows every aspect of our operation and can handle any problem that arises. And yes, he's as honest as the day is long.

Brady grew up and lives just a few miles from Camelot. He worked his way through high school and his first year of college at Chick-fil-A (known for offering some of the best training and service in the entire restaurant industry). He also worked two summers as an apprentice technician for a large HVAC company. A sophomore at Mines, he's not on scholarship, so he's making his own way and helping to foot the bill for his own tuition. In other words, Brady is the poster child for grit, determination, and work ethic.

Your Knights Are Out There, but
You've Gotta Be Willing to Hunt

Take out a pen and paper and write down the title of one of the jobs you're having trouble filling.

Have you depended on fishing as your primary tactic to lure that perfect catch? Are you relying too heavily on "Help Wanted" signs and Craigslist/Indeed-type job boards? Are you throwing tons of random darts and hoping one of them hits a target?

How's that strategy going for you?

My hunch is that if it were going well, you wouldn't be reading this book.

The truth is that you can fish and get lucky. Maybe you once brought in a great employee who drove by and saw your NOW HIRING sign in the window. Or maybe once you hit the lottery and landed a Brady with a low-cost ad on Craigslist.

Heck, even a blind pig can find an acorn every once in a while.

But unless you're paying two to three times more than anyone else in your community, you're not going to be able to find and keep great employees if fishing for talent is your only ploy. There aren't enough fish in that stream.

You may have gotten lucky in the past, but you can't rely on luck. Now it's time to master the hunt.

Hunting Grounds—Go Where the Big Game Is

Hunting for great employees isn't something that should be left up to any one person or department in your organization. Nor is it a chore that should be dropped on HR's doorstep.

In great organizations, every employee, regardless of their position—from part-time custodian up to the chairman of the board—is trained to hunt. Every person knows that their success is based on the success of the organization and that the success of the organization is based on the quality of people it employs. They are unified in their mission to staff the company with the very best people possible.

The biggest problem many business owners, leaders, managers, and supervisors have is that they don't know exactly what they're looking for. When asked what kind of employee they want to hire, they say, "I'm just looking for good people." Or, "I just want someone who's not afraid to work hard."

These kinds of generalities won't generate strong referrals. After all, most everyone you know and choose to associate with could fit the description of "good people" who "work hard." But that doesn't mean they'd be a good fit for the job in question.

To be successful in your hunt, you need to know EXACTLY what you're looking for.

To find Brady, I started with a "magic wand" list. I charted out what the perfect candidate would look like in terms of their skills, abilities, personality, and other essentials (e.g., where they live and what hours they can work). If I hadn't created that list, seeing the "M" on the mountain in Golden wouldn't have resonated with me. I wouldn't have considered hunting for a Mines student who could potentially fill that role.

Start by creating your own a "magic wand" list. If you can't imagine someone being able to check all the boxes, prioritize the most important items first.

Let's say you're hiring for a sous chef. Write out your ideal criteria: The ideal person for this position must be able to bake a soufflé and must be able to work weekend nights. An MBA is a plus.

The deal killer, of course, is if they can't bake a soufflé or can't work weekends. While business savvy comes in handy in the restaurant world, it may not be essential that the candidate have an MBA.

Success Leaves Clues That Lead You to Your Hunting Ground

One of the best and most commonly overlooked strategies for identifying your "target" (the ideal candidate for this job) is to carefully consider current and previous ideal employees you've had in similar positions.

For example, if Rachelle was the best morning cashier you've ever had, list everything you know about her that makes her such a great employee.

What school did she go to, and what courses did she take? What are her particular skills and talents? How did she find this job? Why did this job fit her so well that she excelled in it?

Any and all of these clues can lead you to the ideal hunting ground, where you'll find other Rachelles likely seeking the same kind of opportunities you offer.

The Only Places You'll Find Great People Are the Places You Hunt

Most of this book is devoted to specific steps, tactics, and best practices for finding great people to work for you. Think of each of these chapters as your treasure map or, better yet, your personal guide to talent hunting. I've worked with hundreds of organizations of every imaginable kind and size, in every imaginable industry, and in a variety of geographic locations. Over decades of research and close interaction with corporate teams, I've discovered amazing ideas and strategies for finding very talented and motivated people to do jobs that, well, let's just say not many people dream about.

There's a Brady (or 10 or 50 Bradys) out there who are perfect fits for your business. They can excel in the jobs you're looking to fill, and they want to join your ranks as badly as you want them to work for you.

You've just got to stop thinking that your job-posting bait is enough to bring them in. Instead, you'll need to identify exactly what it is you're looking for, improve your aim, and start to hunt.

But wait. There's one very, very, very, very important thing you must do first.

You see, no matter how skilled you are at hunting, you'll lose great people much faster than you can get them if you aren't a great employer.

So take a deep breath, because here it comes...

It starts with being a great place to work!

Chapter 3

BEFORE YOU HUNT,
Make Your Company
a Great Place to Work

Imagine you just discovered a killer recruiting strategy and recently put it to work at your company. Practically overnight, you begin to see the results of this new strategy, and it's nothing short of astonishing!

Applications are pouring in. And not just applications—applications from qualified, highly experienced candidates who want to work for you. Each one you review impresses you more than the last. You set up a bunch of interviews, and every single applicant shows up on time, neatly attired, résumé in hand. They all interview as if they know EXACTLY what you're looking for and were born to do the jobs you need to fill. They all fit in with your culture hand-in-glove. What's more, they all pass your stringent background checks and drug tests with flying colors, and the references suggest these candidates are heaven sent!

Best recruiting strategy ever, you think. And you hire as many of the candidates as you can as fast as you can so they can start producing for you in a big way.

Two weeks after they've started, you can see that your heaven-sent, big-time producers are the real deal. Killer recruiting strategy indeed!

Everything's perfect. That is, until it isn't. See, just three months after they all start, every single one of these amazing people has up and quit. *What's going on?* you wonder. Most of them aren't asked why they quit, but the few who are say that the work environment wasn't what they had expected. They weren't happy working for you. They got less than they had bargained for. As a result, the entire crew you just brought on has already turned over, and you have to start hunting for replacements all over again.

Too extreme of an example? Maybe. But maybe not.

You've probably suffered through the unexpected turnover of your best and brightest because employees who were the perfect fit for you discovered that your organization wasn't the perfect fit for them. And just like in a marriage, it takes two to tango.

Many leaders and managers have painful memories of searching everywhere to find a Brady. Once found, your Brady was a godsend. You knew that you had found a perfect mutual fit. You believed in your heart that your Brady would be with you for the next 40 years and eventually retire after receiving a standing ovation, celebratory cake, and gold watch in the company cafeteria. Then just two years, two months, two weeks, or maybe only just two days after you said, "You're hired," your Brady disappeared like a butterfly in a tornado. Brady found a better job. Or worse, your Brady left without even having another job lined up. (Reality check: Some Bradys leave because they're pretty sure they can do better just about anywhere else.)

Ouch.

The recruiting section of this book is filled with valuable hiring tactics and best practices, but those tactics and practices will get you only so far. This chapter comes before the recruiting section for a reason. Nothing I tell you from here on out is going to help you become FULLY STAFFED if you can't keep the great people you hire. If your hiring strategy is spot on but your people leave far sooner than you would like, you have a problem.

And the only way to solve that problem and keep great people is to make your company or organization a great place to work.

Few employers I've ever met would admit that their company is a crappy (or at least less-than-ideal) place to work. In fact, most employers believe that their company is a great place to work and that the reason they can't stay FULLY STAFFED is that *there just aren't any good, hardworking people out there anymore. It's tragic really, but that's the state of affairs in today's entitled day and age where people don't know what it's like to put in an honest day's work. They no longer know how to give it their all and show some loyalty by sticking around.*

It's not me (and my great workplace), these employers think. *It's you.*

There's a word for these employers: delusional.

How Stable Is Your Mousetrap?

Let's say the jobs you're looking to fill pay substantially more than you made when you started out. And let's say your company has better working conditions than most of the jobs you've held in your life. Let's also say that you know in your heart that you're a much nicer guy or gal than some of the SOBs you remember working for.

Well, I have news for you. Your life experience doesn't mean a damn thing to the people currently in your crosshairs. The only thing that matters to your people is that their employer treats them better than the companies that employ their friends. Trust me: they know everything there is to know about their friends' employers because their friends talk about their employers all the time. The emerging workforce is more open and transparent than you could possibly imagine about their jobs, their company, their compensation package, and the way they're treated by their superiors.

What good would it be to try to catch mice by spending lavishly on the best cheese in the world only to set that cheese in a trap with a broken spring and a latch made of tissue paper? The mice would come in droves and quickly make off with the pricey cheese. You'd go broke before ever catching a mouse.

Your ability to achieve FULLY STAFFED status doesn't end with the hunt (attracting and recruiting good people). You must be equally skilled at the keep (employee retention).

Dude, We're a Small Outfit, Not Google!

Even if they don't top the list of *Fortune Magazine*'s 100 BEST PLACES TO WORK, Google is always among the top 5. Shocker, right?

Okay, maybe not. Google pays outrageously high starting wages. Their main campus in Mountain View, California, offers employees free meals at any one of nine company cafeterias, and those meals are prepared by a team of executive chefs. In addition to the perks and benefits that most big companies offer employees, Googlers get free car washes, child care, laundry and dry cleaning services, massages, elaborate exercise facilities, nap time… the list goes on and on and on.

I know what you're thinking.

"Hey dude, I just run a _____. I'm not Google!"
insert type of business here

Relax. The good news is that you don't have to be.

You just need to be a better _____ than your
insert type of business here
competitor.

In this scenario, your competitor could be the same kind of business or a business in the same industry. Or your competitor could be a radically different kind of business in a totally different industry.

Your competitor is any business or organization that you're losing your best people to.

Let's say you run GIZMO Peanut Butter Recycling. If a significant number of your people are quitting your company to work for ACME Peanut Butter Recycling, then ACME has something you don't. The first step in putting your finger in the leaky bucket is to identify the 100 percent unvarnished truth as to why your people are leaving for ACME.

That means you need to exit interview everyone who leaves of their own accord. Call them in, thank them for their service, and ask them if they'll help you build a better place to work for their former colleagues and the people who will eventually replace them. Take notes, and do your very best to limit yourself to 10 percent of the talking so they can fill in the other 90 percent. Don't dispute anything they say, even if it isn't accurate. If they say they're leaving because they hate the rock-and-roll music you blare in the cafeteria and you don't even have a sound system, smile warmly and say, "Thank you, I appreciate your sharing that. What other changes can we make here at GIZMO to keep good employees like you?"

Although it's possible that you're losing your people to ACME because they pay more than you can offer, it's also very likely that money isn't the only reason they're leaving—or even the primary reason.

The problem could boil down to your culture.

You Can't Fix Your Culture if You Don't Know What's Broken

Culture is a term so frequently tossed around in today's lexicon that it's easy to feel kinda stupid if you don't know what everyone's talking about when they use it in the context of business. Essentially, culture, as it applies to your company or workplace, simply means how your employees truly feel about working for you, how they make decisions that guide their actions, and how they go about their jobs on a typical workday.

In the Great Depression, employers didn't give a damn about their culture. They didn't have to. Far more people were looking for work than there were jobs available. Employees who didn't like their boss, or their workplace conditions, or their paycheck, or the way they were treated kept their mouths shut because they knew a long line of hungry, out-of-work people would have happily taken their job. Employers had all the power and held all the cards.

Today, the tide hasn't just changed; it has completely reversed.

As opposed to in a depressed economy or even one in a deep recession, in today's economy culture has become crucial to your ability to attract and retain people. Today's PERFECT STORM has changed who's doing the demanding and who's doing the groveling. Understandably, employers like you aren't thrilled about that. Nonetheless, it's time to accept the reality of the situation. Your company will be a great place to work, or you won't keep good people. It's as simple as that.

How to Create a Culture of Employees Who Are ON FIRE for You

My 2015 book, *On Fire at Work: How Great Companies Ignite Passion in Their People Without Burning Them Out*, includes a deep dive into the topic of workplace culture. In my research for that book, I interviewed the founders, CEOs, and presidents of more than 25 celebrated companies frequently cited as the "best places to work" in their respective industries. My goal was to highlight the ideas and strategies that leading organizations use to get the very best from the people they employ and what those companies are doing to retain them.

In that book, rather than looking at hiring and retention from the employer's perspective, I've flipped the equation to try to see the situation through the lens of today's workforce. If you want to hire people who possess both hard "technical" skills and soft "work ethic" skills, you need to know what these people are demanding from today's employers. What do they want?

The answer to this question seems simple on the surface, but the number of companies that exemplify the combination of these elements are few and far between.

Regardless of the industry, size of the business, or geographic location, your employees need seven things—let's call them cultural pillars—to remain engaged and perform up to their potential. In random order, these pillars are as follows:

- **COMPENSATION** – money, perks, benefits, and work-life balance
- **ALIGNMENT** – meaningful work at a company with values that mirror their own
- **GROWTH** – opportunities to learn new skills and advance in their careers
- **ATMOSPHERE** – a workplace that provides a safe, upbeat, enjoyable experience
- **ACKNOWLEDGMENT** – feeling appreciated, rewarded, and sometimes even celebrated
- **AUTONOMY** – encouragement to think and act independently and make decisions
- **COMMUNICATION** – being informed about relevant company issues and knowing the company is actively listening to their ideas in the pursuit of honest feedback

The acid test to determine the validity of these cultural pillars is quite simply a role reversal.

Imagine that you've lost your job and you find yourself looking for work. A friend tells you that you have the perfect skill set for an opening at their company and that they can get you an interview for a position that's nearly identical to the one you just vacated. It sounds too good to be true, but, filled with optimism, you begin to prepare for the interview.

Along the way, you discover that the position hits six of the pillars but is severely deficient in the seventh.

The salary is less than half what you were making before and not enough to sustain your current lifestyle without drastic changes. Or the salary is terrific, but you learn this company has repeatedly been fined for pouring toxic chemicals into your town's water supply. Or the company pays well and is very ethical, but an overwhelming number of reviews on Glassdoor indicate that employees are micromanaged and forced to submit minute-by-minute personal productivity reports to their supervisor.

Which of the seven pillars would *you* be willing to sacrifice?

Naturally, if you were desperate for a job, you'd be more willing to compromise here and there. But assuming your skills are in high demand and you have an impressive list of references from previous employers, which of the pillars would you scratch off the list?

Probably not even one. While you might rank the pillars differently according to your specific needs and desires, you wouldn't be excited about going to work for any organization where one or more of these pillars is missing.

Your Company Is Constantly Being Judged Against These Seven Pillars

Every current employee and any prospective employee you're hoping to attract expect all seven of these cultural pillars to be present and prioritized in their job. The more skilled and talented those employees are, the more in-demand they are in the marketplace, and the more they will expect from each pillar.

Let's say you just won a big construction bid and need to hire certified masons. If the contractor down the street is willing to pay masons more than you can afford, they likely win on the COMPENSATION pillar. But just because you lost the compensation battle doesn't necessarily mean you've lost the labor war. The way to win the labor war is to attract and keep the best masons by offering a better workplace on at least five to six of the other cultural pillars.

For example, you might win on the GROWTH pillar because you offer full tuition reimbursement for masons who take approved management courses, something your competitor doesn't do. You might win on the ALIGNMENT pillar because your masons can take one Friday off each month if they agree to use at least 50 percent of that day helping to build or repair homes for economically disadvantaged people in your community. You might win on the COMMUNICATION pillar because each mason on your crew is taken to lunch by a supervisor or superintendent once a month and asked to share their candid thoughts about how a particular project is going and how the company can improve the quality of their products and services and increase sales and customer satisfaction.

What the Great Ones Have in Common

The business owners, leaders, managers, and companies that are serious about employee engagement and retention are relentless in their pursuit to be the best place to work in their industry and community. They don't simply decide to give each employee a free turkey before Thanksgiving and think, "That should do it. We win!" Rather, they're always looking for ways they can improve on each pillar, and they leave no stone unturned.

The companies and leaders who are thriving as FULLY STAFFED organizations are those that consistently have their ear to the ground to listen to their people and anticipate their needs and desires. They study other employers in their industry, along with employers in very different industries, in an attempt to glean fresh ideas and new strategies that can boost employee engagement and make their company more employee focused.

If you lost your current job or the company you own was zapped to another dimension by an alien gamma ray, you'd eventually have to find another job.

What company would YOU want to work for? And more importantly, why?

You would probably choose a company you've heard good things about. You would probably choose a company known for treating their people like gold, a company strong on most or all of those seven cultural pillars.

You see, news travels fast, and it travels far.

Bad places to work have bad reputations. Current and former employees will tell everyone they know to steer clear of a bad workplace.

On the other hand, everyone wants to work at a great place that has a great reputation. Google receives between two and three million applications every year—some estimate 50,000 applications per week—and many of those applicants have degrees from the world's most prestigious colleges and universities or have experience working for the world's most prestigious companies. Google is a great place to work, so they can afford to be very, very picky about whom they choose to hire.

In an effort to avoid toxic or bad hires, Google applicants are generally subjected to a grueling 12-step interview process. Based on the ratio of applicants to hires, landing a job at Google is roughly ten times more difficult than getting into Harvard.

What would happen if you subjected your applicants to more than one interview? Would they disappear before the second? Can you afford to be choosy and select among a large pool of applicants, or do you end up settling for anyone who agrees to take the job and passes a drug test?

As I said, you don't have to be Google. However, the better the culture you offer your employees, the more your company will stand out from the pack. The more you stand out, the more applications you will receive from qualified candidates. The more applications you receive by being a great place to work, the less you'll have to recruit to become FULLY STAFFED with the best possible people.

Don't get me wrong. Even with 50,000 applications pouring in each week, Google still recruits. And having a better mousetrap (a workplace culture with seven strong cultural pillars) does help bring in the best applicants and definitely helps you keep the best people.

But that's only half the solution to your problem.

To be FULLY STAFFED throughout this perfect storm, you've got to be a better hunter than your competitors, and you need to know where and how to hunt.

Everyone who works for you needs to join you in this hunt. And they need to be trained and skilled for this hunt.

That's what the next section—most of this book—is dedicated to.

Ready? Let's go hunting...

PART 2

FINDING GREAT EMPLOYEES

Chapter 4

1960 CALLED
And Wants Its
"Help Wanted" Sign Back

In one episode of the old television classic *The Andy Griffith Show*, Opie (Andy's prepubescent son, played by a young Ron Howard before he became a famous Hollywood director) wants a guitar. His "Pa," Andy Griffith, tells Opie he's going to have to find a way to earn the money to buy it.

A few days later, Opie sees a "Help Wanted" sign in the window of Crawford's Drugstore and runs in to apply. Naturally, Mr. Crawford hires Opie, and after a few snafus everything works out wonderfully—just as it always did in the town of Mayberry back in the 1960s.

Although *The Andy Griffith Show* is a fictional story set in a fictional place, there actually was a time when all an employer had to do was post a "Help Wanted" sign on the door in order to draw in a bunch of qualified candidates and hire great people.

Them Mayberry days are gone.

Unlike Mr. Crawford, you can't rely on a "Help Wanted" sign to keep your business FULLY STAFFED. But that doesn't mean you shouldn't advertise job openings with signs, banners, and postings that are visible to your patrons, customers, vendors, suppliers, and really, all passersby. There's always a chance, and perhaps a darn good one, that a well-written, strategically placed sign advertising an opening at your business will attract someone who's a great long-term fit.

Don't get me wrong. I'm not suggesting that you go full-on old school, scribbling "Help Wanted" or "Now Hiring" on a sheet of paper and taping that sheet to the nearest wall. If you want to maximize the odds that an on-premise sign will work for you, you're going to want to post the right sign for your business in the right place.

And make no mistake, you're going to want to do everything you can to maximize your odds. Simply put, advertising job openings to people who frequent your place of business is the easiest, fastest, and most affordable way to alert others to the opportunities you have available.

That's *why* you should use on-premise signs and postings.

Now let's focus on *who* you should direct your signs to, *what* your signs should say, *when* you should post your signs, *where* your signs should be posted, and *how* prospective applicants—or someone who knows prospective applicants—should take action.

WHO Your Signs Should Target

Let's return to the "magic wand" question posed in Chapter 2. For the specific job openings you're trying to fill, who's *your* Brady?

Are you searching for:

- Happy, smiling people who are eager to provide above-and-beyond service to your customers?

- Hard-working, organized, introverted self-starters willing to work the graveyard shift?

- Certified craftspeople who like to travel and work independently with minimal supervision?

- Gregarious call center staff who enjoy talking to people on the phone?

The perfect fits for each of these positions differ dramatically. If you use a catch-all "Help Wanted" sign (ideal qualifications: someone who's breathing), you'll waste valuable time sorting through bad fits and possibly miss the needle in that haystack.

Start by being intentional. The pickier you are about WHO you're looking for, the easier it will be to find them.

This advice may sound counterintuitive. You may be thinking, "Dude, I'm trying to fill some mighty unsexy jobs. I need to take anyone who applies because beggars can't be choosers." But that's a self-fulfilling prophecy—if you convince yourself you need to settle, you're going to settle. This kind of thinking is dangerous and limiting, and it's keeping you from identifying and attracting your perfect fits. In this murky labor pond, you won't find your Bradys, and your Bradys won't know how to find you.

Start by writing out your "magic wand" criteria. Carefully examine the specific tasks you need performed, the working conditions associated with the position, and the traits of the people who excel in this position. The clearer you are in your own mind, the better.

Now that you know who you're going after, you can determine WHAT your signage needs to say to get their attention.

WHAT Your Signs Should Say

At Modern Market, a trendy, fast-casual eatery, I recently noticed a sign that stopped me in my tracks.

PREPARING AMAZING FOOD FROM SCRATCH IS HARD

We're Looking for People Who Relish That Challenge and Want to Help Us Change the Way Americans Eat

Whoa! This sign is quite a departure from the typical *Join Our Team* signs you see at just about every other restaurant these days. But then, Modern Market obviously isn't looking for people who will work at any old place. Modern Market knows their unique value proposition, and they incorporate that proposition into their signage. They're deliberately reaching out to people who connect with their brand identity and mission.

Think about it. You're a customer who's picky about what you eat. You pop into Modern Market for lunch. Even if you have zero interest in working at a restaurant, you nonetheless learn (1) they're hiring, and (2) they won't hire just anyone. They're looking for people seeking a challenge, change, and better health—people who share their values.

If you're looking for a job or career opportunity in the restaurant industry *and* you won't settle for the first job you can find, THIS could be the sign you've been looking for. (Even if it's not the job for you, it might be the job for your hardworking, health-conscious mother, brother, daughter, nephew, or neighbor. After seeing this sign, the chances are good that you'll spread the word.)

Your on-premise employment marketing should appeal to the wants, needs, hopes, and dreams of your ideal fit. Once you determine who your ideal fit is, ask yourself what *they* want in a job, and make sure your sign appeals to them.

And be original. The Modern Market sign would be laughable if it were posted at a burger chain or a four-star French bistro. It just wouldn't fit—and it wouldn't draw in the right kinds of candidates.

Of course, with regard to content, shorter is better. No one's going to read your book-length "Help Wanted" sign. You've got to get to the point and get there fast. Use graphics when possible or consider including a photo of someone doing the job you're hiring for. That way, prospects can actually visualize themselves in that role.

In some situations, it may be better to advertise what your job openings *aren't* rather than what they *are*. My five kids each worked their way through high school at various fast food restaurants, and I vividly remember their complaints about how the grease would cause breakouts, how they didn't like dealing with rude drive-through customers, and how the weekend midnight shifts would throw their sleep schedule into a whirl. I recently noticed a sign in the window of a neighborhood Subway restaurant that reads:

NOW HIRING COOL PEOPLE
NO LATE NIGHTS
NO DRIVE THRU
NO GREASE

My kids would have applied in a heartbeat. Talk about setting your brand apart from others.

What can your employees say about working for you that they couldn't say if they were employed by your competitor? That's a good place to start when you're looking to articulate your brand difference and employment advantage.

I have one more key point to share about WHAT to say. Many employers lead with a headline about the wages they offer ("Our drivers start at $18 per hour!"). Money may be an effective way to draw applicants in, but those applicants are usually seeing dollar signs, not the other reasons why they should be excited about taking the job and working for your company. And if they get wind that the place down the street pays drivers $19 per hour, BAM! They'll be gone faster than you can rip up your $18 per hour sign and replace it with one that advertises your new hourly rate of $20.

Some of the best signs appeal to applicants' core values, not to their wallet. For example, most every school district in the United States is desperate to hire school bus drivers. (Make no mistake, it takes more than a paycheck to inspire any sane adult to drive around a busload of screaming kids or cranky teens.) Rather than advertise the wage offered, many districts are posting signs like this one that appeal to the public service nature of the job:

BECOME THE DRIVING FORCE IN THE EDUCATION OF OUR YOUTH

"Punny" signs like this one hit home with people who want to make a difference in their community. And if those people can make a difference *and* make money—all the better.

Before creating your signage, ask yourself, ask your fellow leaders, and definitely ask your staff the following question: "What is truly unique about this business from the perspective of the people we're looking to hire for the _____ position?"

Listen to what they have to say, and then channel their thoughts and ideas to appeal to the people searching for that very kind of opportunity.

WHEN to Post Your Signs

Imagine that a prospective superstar—someone highly skilled with a killer work ethic—is in your lobby or driving by your business right now. If that superstar doesn't see any indication that you need their skills, he or she might just go to work for your competitor. Big loss for you. Big win for your competitor. Double whammy!

If the only time your "Now Hiring" sign comes out is when you have an urgent need (e.g., "My three best installers just quit on me!"), then you'll always be in panic hiring mode. Panic hiring mode makes you a beggar, not a chooser. You've been there, done that. Enough's enough.

If you want to stay FULLY STAFFED, you need to interview and recruit full time, all the time. One of my favorite axioms is "Plan ahead. It wasn't raining when Noah built the ark."

Great athletic teams are always on the lookout for talent to upgrade their rosters, and none of them would ever shy away from bringing on a prospect with outstanding potential even if they already have a superstar starting in that position and a full bench. And great players, in turn, know they must continue to perform at a high level. They know any of those guys on the bench licking their chops on the sidelines would gladly take their place.

It's the same with great companies and organizations, big and small. They're always hunting for great talent. The days of "Sorry, we're not hiring" are gone. Possibly forever.

Here's a little test. Let's say you look over your team roster and each name brings a smile to your face. There's not a thing in the world you would change. Great! Can't you finally take down those hiring signs?

You know the answer. Keep piling up those applications, and keep conducting interviews. It will help you better understand what sorts of employees you're seeking and keep you FULLY STAFFED for the long haul. It will also make your staff aware that others out there are hungry for their jobs and are simply waiting for a window of opportunity. I'd call that a "performance motivator."

WHERE to Post Your Signs

To succeed, your signs need to be seen by your prospective "perfect fit" targets. The more you know about those prospects and where they walk, drive, shop, eat, etc., the more effective you'll be at getting your message in front of them.

The funniest, most dramatic, or most compelling product ads ever created would crash and burn if they appeared in the wrong media. That's why you'll never see an ad featuring the new lineup of BMWs in *The National Enquirer*, a coupon for a "buy one, get one free" Whopper in *Cosmopolitan*, or a commercial for tampons during a televised Ultimate Fighting Championship cage match. Placing even the best-designed ads in the wrong media outlets means targeted buyers aren't likely to see them.

Driving down the interstate, you'll notice that more than half of the commercial trucks now post job openings on the sides or backs of their cargo compartments. The signs point out the advantages of driving for that particular company and tell other truck drivers—who might be less than thrilled with their present employers—how to apply.

You can determine *where* to place your ads only after you identify your "perfect fit" prospect. Once you know the *who*, then you can find the perfect *where*. Below are some examples of employers who found the ideal place to position their signs:

Steven Johns of Envisioning Green, a landscaping company in Caseyville, Illinois, realized that more than 75 percent of his workforce came from the same six-block radius. He came up with the idea to post yard signs on local medians and intersections. As a result, he generated an immediate 30 percent increase in applications.

Jeff Richardson, owner of JK Insulation located in Southern California, places large signs advertising openings on company trucks and then parks them where they are clearly visible by passing traffic during off-hours and weekends.

At Golling Chrysler Dodge Jeep Ram in Bloomfield Hills, Michigan, the service center team places stickers on the oil filters they install that promote the job opportunities and advantages Golling offers. So when the owner of the car brings it in for an oil change at another oil and lube center, the tech is going to see that sticker, and they might be tempted to check out the job opportunities at Golling.

Steve Reisenberg, a ProSource dealer in Erie, Pennsylvania, had a sign made, similar to one used when selling a house, that read "Account Manager Opening—Apply Within," and placed the sign on the lawn in front of their location. He said his sign attracts several candidates each month.

Posting bilingual "For Hire" signs in laundry mats, bodegas, and other places near the main office has worked well for Christa Mruz, who owns a Two Maids and a Mop franchise in White Plains, New York. She also keeps a posting at a local center that assists Hispanic people and immigrants to find employment.

Roger Panitch, owner of a College H.U.N.K.S. Hauling Junk & Moving® franchise in Atlanta, made his "Help Wanted" signs into a "You're Amazing at Work. We Should Talk"-formatted business card that he and his team pass out when they see someone who they believe would be a great fit for their business. The back of this card outlines the benefits of working for his company and also states, "You've provided excellent service. If you're looking for an opportunity or want to make a change, we'd like to talk to you."

Becky Pelle, owner of a Blackjack Pizza franchise in Loveland, Colorado, posted a sign on the curb that read, "Fully staffed and ready to serve you." Numerous people applied for a job within the first two weeks and she removed the sign. Says Becky: "I believe 'fully staffed' meant a great place to work."

Using the sign on a tip jar to advertise job openings is how Deke and Jen Gillies attract potential employees to their Aroma Joe's coffee franchise in Gray Village, Maine.

At a new restaurant opening for a Freddy's Steakburger and Custard restaurant, Kyle Gerstner, owner of nine Freddy's, dispatched his management team to blanket the local outdoor walking mall with their unique version of "Now Hiring" flyers. But the team didn't just leave the flyers and walk away. Instead, they remained nearby to notice which shoppers stopped to read the flyers and then to strike up conversations with those who appeared interested.

The lesson here is to take your message *where* it's going to have maximum visibility for the people you really want to see it.

HOW Prospective Employees Should Take Action

Let's say you're the owner of the local Soup-n-Sandwich Shack franchise. Marcus, your perfect-fit prospect, passes by on his way to a job he doesn't love and reads your "Now Hiring" sign. "WOW!" he thinks. "Soup-n-Sandwich Shack is awesome! The job they're advertising is exactly the job I'm looking for!"

Good news for you! So now what? What is Marcus supposed to do next?

Marcus checks the sign for contact information and sees a URL. Sweet! Unfortunately, that URL is www.soupnsandwichshack.com/chicago /store5745/career-jobs/1536-parkerstreet. That's gonna be a tough one to remember. He snaps a picture with his phone. That afternoon, after multiple attempts to enter the website address correctly, he finally reaches the right webpage but can't find a link that takes him to an online application. He does, however, find the store's phone number. He calls and reaches an employee, who tells him, "Whoa, I think we've already got a full staff, but I'll take a message just for the heck of it." She throws his call into voicemail. A recorded voice tells him, "Mailbox full."

Let's just say that Marcus is pretty resourceful and he really wants to work at your restaurant. Forget the website, forget the phone—he's ready to leave his current job. So the next day he marches into your establishment and asks Lashondra, the young woman behind the counter, for an application. "Are you the dude who called yesterday?" she asks. "I'm the only one here now. You're going to have to come back in a few hours when the boss is here. She's out running errands."

Not one to give up, Marcus asks Lashondra for a job application. She gives him a blank look. "Can you at least tell the manager I stopped by?" he asks.

"What am I supposed to tell her?" she asks.

He writes his name and phone number on the back of a paper menu and hands it to her. "I'm here for a job," he says. "Please ask the manager or the person who does the hiring to call me."

After Marcus leaves, Lashondra shrugs and sets the menu atop a pile of papers under the counter. You return from running errands an hour later. "Anything I need to know about?" you ask her.

"Ummm, not really. But it's been a little busy and we ran out of onions," she says.

Here's what just happened in a nutshell. Marcus could have been the best employee you've had in years. He was more than qualified, and he really wanted to work for you. He was someone who could think outside the box—someone who always followed up and followed through.

And you caught him in your net...only, your net had a huge hole, and now he's gone forever.

What if every Marcus you hired was worth thousands of dollars—or potentially tens of thousands of dollars—to your company? What if the continued success of your business hinged on employing people like Marcus? What would it take for you to sit up and take notice? If Marcus owned a business on the next block and he wanted to use your restaurant to cater his weekly lunch-n-learn for a dozen clients, and his business was worth thousands of dollars to you, would you have made sure that Lashondra knew exactly how to accommodate his request? Would you have taken every possible precaution to make sure there were no holes in your net?

Absolutely. Without a doubt. You need customers to stay in business. And just as important, you need great employees to serve those customers. And they must not only be able to increase sales and perform their jobs; they also need to be well schooled on how to help you reel in any job seekers who respond to your on-premise employment postings.

Make certain your signage gives applicants simple, straightforward, no-friction steps to follow. Ditch the crazy URLs and voicemail. Train your employees on how to support your hiring efforts so they never send a key prospect packing. If someone sees your sign on Saturday, don't make them wait until Monday to apply. And if someone sees your sign on Saturday and applies on Monday, don't make them wait until two weeks from Friday to get a response. If a prospective superstar takes the initiative to knock on your door, the very least you can do is answer it and welcome them in.

You must streamline your hiring process and make applying for your open positions a total no-brainer if you want to be FULLY STAFFED. And this no-brainer process needs to be clearly stated on your signs. The point is simple: streamline the hiring process, and guide prospects every step of the way. Don't settle for simply making it easy for candidates to get every detail right. Instead, *make it impossible for them to get anything wrong.*

Tips and Tactics

Your on-premise signs and postings can attract no one (a big problem), attract everyone (another big problem), or solve many of your problems by attracting the right people in the right way. Follow these tips and tactics to determine *why* you should post signs, *who* you should direct your signs to, *what* your signs should say, *when* you should post your signs, *where* your signs should be posted, and *how* prospective applicants should take action:

- Accept the WHY. Advertising job openings to people who frequent your place of business is the easiest, fastest, and most affordable way to alert others to the opportunities you have available.

- Start by being intentional. Write out your "magic wand" criteria for each open position. The pickier you are about WHO you're looking for, the easier it will be to find them.

- Ensure your on-premise employment marketing appeals to the wants, needs, hopes, and dreams of your ideal fit. Once you determine who your ideal fit is, ask yourself WHAT they want in a job, and make sure your sign appeals to them.

- Post "Help Wanted" signs on an ongoing basis if you want to stay FULLY STAFFED. WHEN should you be interviewing and recruiting? The answer: all the time.

- Determine WHERE to place your ads only after you identify your "perfect fit" prospect. Once you know the who, then you can find the perfect where.

- Accept the fact that you'll have a much greater chance of being FULLY STAFFED if you streamline your hiring process and show candidates HOW to take next steps by making the application process a total no-brainer.

Chapter 5

EMPLOYEE REFERRALS
Get Your A-Team Recruiting for You

When I was in high school, I had all the typical high school jobs: mowing lawns, washing dishes, working in a fast food restaurant. Wherever I worked, my managers went out of their way not to hire my friends for fear we'd spend too much time talking and goofing off.

When I was 17, I got a job at a high-fashion men's store in a mall in Lakewood, Colorado. A friend of mine also wanted to work there, but I knew the manager wouldn't give him a chance if he knew we were buddies. So Mike and I concocted a plan for how he could get hired. I told him everything he needed to know: how to dress, what to say, what questions he would be asked in the interview, and what hours he should request. In addition, I tipped him off as to my manager's likes and dislikes. Most importantly, Mike knew that he had to act as if he didn't know me. Sure enough, he applied, got an interview, and followed that plan. Boom! Mike was hired.

Working with my buddy made the retail hours fly by and made working at this store a lot more fun. And yes, we did horse around a bit and got into some harmless mischief. (Let's just say we weren't supervised as closely as 17-year-olds probably should be.) But we also outperformed most of our peers, and our boss grew to really like both of us.

Times Have Changed

Employer fears of chaotic, unproductive friendship pairings at work aren't baseless, of course. Some people, regardless of their age, aren't capable of working side by side with their friends like responsible adults. But the only reason for hiring or retaining such childish, irresponsible people is out of desperation, and this chapter is a step-by-step instruction guide to replacing desperation with a solid plan of action. Referrals from your best and brightest employees are one of your best sources for identifying exceptional candidates. Period.

The best companies in the United States recognize this truth, which is why my artful plan to get my good friend hired is a dramatic departure from what goes on at businesses today. Business owners and hiring managers love to hire their employees' friends because it's a win-win for the company and for the employees. Having friends in the workplace increases employee engagement and satisfaction. It also gives employees extra incentive to show up and support each other's success on the job. That is why one of the 12 questions asked on the renowned Q12 Employee Engagement Survey from the Gallup Organization is "Do you have a best friend at work?"

Employee referral programs are an extremely common and useful way to recruit and hire quickly. The concept is simple. Ask employees you trust if they have any friends who need a job. If they refer someone, you reward them. It's a great setup, one that maximizes output with the least amount of effort on your part.

However, if you want your employee referrals to really hit the mark, you'll need to walk before you run. Remember the two most important prerequisites:

1. Be a great place to work.
2. Refer back to rule one—nothing in this book will work if you ignore rule one.

Want excellent referrals from your employees? First build a desirable workplace. It's that simple.

Ambiguity Will Get You Nowhere. Be Specific.

Once your company is attracting great people inside and out, then you can focus on developing your referral program. You must be extremely clear in defining your hiring goals. Clarity is of the utmost importance when asking your employees to recruit for you.

Many managers ask their employees something like this: "Hey, can you help me find six people who would do this job?"

These managers are basically asking for six warm bodies. Their hiring criteria? Ideally all six of them should be breathing.

Instead, try telling your employees this: "I'm looking to bring on up to six guys who aren't afraid to pick up a shovel, who can work long days or overnight shifts, who won't mind getting dirty, and who can handle the elements. They don't need a college degree or even a high school diploma, but they do need to show up on time, and they need a positive attitude. Most importantly, I need guys with a strong back and a work ethic to match."

You're not just looking for people who want to work—you're also looking for team members. When your vision for what you want is clear, the directive to your employees must be equally clear.

Instead of telling Kylie, your star employee, to "go find me some people," say, "Kylie, I really appreciate your work ethic and your knowledge of the way we do things here at our company. Do you know anyone who might be as easy to work with as you? I'm looking for people who have a great head on their shoulders like you, and it would be fantastic if they're as friendly and adaptable as you are."

See the difference?

A while back I delivered a presentation for Signal 88, a growing franchise that offers a full suite of security services to commercial, residential, retail, and institutional customers across the United States. I had a chance to speak with one of the franchise owners, who prefers the face-to-face approach to getting employee referrals.

Chris, the franchisee, told me, "I approach my best employees and tell them they're doing really well in their jobs. I then ask them if they happen to know anyone else like them who needs a good, solid job.

"They think for a second, and you can almost see a light bulb appear above their heads. They immediately think of someone, and suddenly—boom—their best friend is working here. Best of all, that friend almost always shares the same strong work ethic because they don't want to work alongside a slouch who would make them look bad.

"Don't ask for referrals by text or e-mail. Do it face to face. That's what really makes an employee want to take extra steps to help you. Everyone has so many connections. It's ridiculous not to tap into them."

Now, once your employees really understand who you're looking for, you need to train them on how to approach prospects. Give them the tools they need to help them achieve the best results. That way, both you and your employee will use time efficiently.

Try a role-playing exercise. Pretend you're the employee's friend, the referral candidate. Ask the employee to approach you with information about the open position. Listen closely and then help the employee fine-tune their language so that they can clearly articulate the responsibilities and qualifications of the job and the ways in which the candidate might be a great fit.

Keeping a referral program in tip-top shape comes down to training. Give yourself the best chances of getting what you want by giving your employees pointed feedback when referrals are up to your standards—and when they're not. Praise employees when they bring you an all-star. Realign your team if they're consistently bringing you duds.

If you interview an employee referral and don't end up hiring that person for one reason or another, always circle back and have a conversation with the employee who did the referring. Realignment is important if you want to build a strong referral program.

Western Water Works (WWW) is Southern California and Utah's premier distributor of pipes, valves, and fittings for the waterworks industry. WWW President Bruce Himes arms his employees with flyers that they can give to their friends and prospective employees. These colorful flyers do the following:

- Outline the reasons why the employee has approached the prospect.

- Highlight what the company is looking for.

- Encourage the prospect to reach out to get more information.

These flyers have an eye-catching design, a powerful message, and clear next steps. Best of all, they maximize employee efficiency. Employees simply hand someone a flyer, and the ball is now in the prospect's court.

It's an easy, genius idea. And it works!

The takeaway: Give your employees a clear referral directive and then train them so well that recruiting becomes second nature.

The VIP Treatment

Speaking of making things easy, when you get referrals from your employees, you need to make sure those referrals are your top priority if you want to be FULLY STAFFED.

If an employee sends you a candidate, don't let that candidate get caught up in your company's hiring bureaucracy. Make sure they aren't buried in the mix of applications submitted online—you don't want their applications lost or shelved by HR. And for Pete's sake, make sure the candidate isn't passed over for an unknown entity walking in the door. Instead, give those referrals a special phone number to call or a special code to enter when applying online. In other words, give them special treatment. You might even make sure that all referral applications land directly on your desk.

Make it **EASY** for your employees' referrals to apply. Let them in through the velvet rope, and then give them a backstage pass. Your employees will see that you really care about their referrals. The more you care, the more your employees will care, and the more great people they'll bring you.

Also be sure to go out of your way to maintain open lines of communication. If you've been waiting on a package from Amazon, you want to be able to track it from the warehouse to your doorstep. Your people and the applicants they refer want the same transparency—they want to know what's going on at every stage of the application and hiring process. Share as much information as you can with both parties.[1] If Joan and Steve both know that Steve's application is next in line, both of them

---

1   Some regional privacy laws limit communications between employer and referrer and referee. In the interests of transparency, go out of your way to share as much information as legally possible with all parties.

will likely have a much more positive experience with the entire referral process. That's just one more way you can demonstrate special treatment in your referral program.

I didn't think seasonal businesses would find employee referrals very lucrative since many seasonal employees are transient, but Bob Prosser changed my opinion. Bob is the owner of the Ishnala Supper Club, located in the Wisconsin Dells, and he approaches employee referrals with old-school special handling techniques. His wildly successful seasonal supper club is open only from early May through the end of October, and in March of each year he sends applications to the team members he wants to bring back. In addition, he sends two extra applications to those all-star employees so they can recruit their A-list friends. The all-star employees then return all three applications so Bob knows who referred whom. Each season, he ends up with a bank of rock stars from which to choose.

Says Bob, "My people don't refer slouches because they know it will reflect poorly on them. They know my expectations, so I can trust their referrals. I would say that 90 percent of my staff comes from these referrals. And there's no monetary bonus for referrals. The bonus is in knowing that you're going to have quality co-workers. Rather than offering money, I offer the best culture."

BIG WIN.

Know Your ABCs

Let's say you've built a great place to work. Your business is growing, and you need more employees, STAT. You blast out an e-mail to your entire staff asking for referrals, and voila, just like that you end up doubling your workforce. Win, right?

Maybe. But possibly not. Here's why.

See, you've got your A-team, or your **Alpha workers**. They're the people in your workforce who work hard, work well with everyone, think outside the box, and help your business thrive.

Then you have your B-team, your **Bravo workers**. They probably make up the majority of your workforce. While they're not rock stars, they're dependable and get their jobs done with little to no maintenance.

Then you've got your C-team, your **Charlie workers**. These third stringers need coaching. They may have intermittent disciplinary issues or occasionally arrive late to work, but otherwise they're fairly manageable. They aren't your go-to task force, but with a little help they work out just fine.

Last, you have your D-team, your **Delta workers**. These are the most volatile and unpredictable people on your team. Sometimes they're good. Sometimes they're awful. They've been pulled into their share of disciplinary meetings and have been written up more than once. They can best be described as your problem children.

Referral Psychology and Crab Mentality

Understanding referral psychology is important because employee referrals don't always work out the way you might think. It turns out that not all employee referrals are created equal.

In a recent study, Lauren Hewitt, a strategic insights analyst for the car service provider Uber, says it's important to assess who's referring whom when it comes to getting your referrals right. Hewitt's research cross-references employee review data with employee referral data. The results are surprising.

For starters, it turns out that Alphas will bring in Alphas. Shocker, right? Okay, maybe not. But here's the first kicker: Bravos generally refer Charlies. Let me restate that in case you missed it—Bravos tend not to refer Alphas or even other Bravos. Bravos tend to refer Charlies.

Why? It comes down to the "crabs in a bucket mentality." Crab mentality can be summarized like this: while any one crab in a bucket can easily escape, other crabs will undermine that crab's efforts, leading to the group's collective demise. In other words, members of a group will try to hold back any member who achieves success beyond the others out of envy, resentment, or spite.

Bravo psychology leads many of them to avoid referring anyone who might outshine them. In a nutshell, be careful when assessing your Bravo referrals because they may not be the "best of the best."

By extension, you might expect Charlies to refer Deltas. Well, here's the second kicker: Charlie referrals run the gamut from Alphas to Bravos to Charlies. Yep, you heard that right. Hewitt theorizes that Charlies aren't as tuned in to the company culture and are therefore likely to bring in anyone they think might work out.

Hewitt doesn't offer statistics on Deltas, but in my opinion it's probably best to put those referrals near the bottom of your list due to a simple lack of predictability. Predictability is key to the success of your referral program. If you can't guess what type of referral an employee might make, it might be best to completely avoid those candidates when you can.[2]

---

2   In some states, you must open up referral programs to your entire staff or risk being in violation of the law. For more information, please consult your state and local regulations regarding employee referral program disclosure.

Great Guys and Gals Hang Out with Great Guys and Gals

Pretend for a moment that you'll be re-interviewing your entire workforce. Think about it—you know exactly who you would hire again on the spot. You might hesitate before rehiring some others. And others might not make the cut.

If the axiom passed down through the years is true, people are most likely to associate with people who are like them. Thus, your top performers are more likely to refer people who would also be top performers. The same could be said for your bottom performers referring other bottom performers. Understanding referral psychology is an essential element in maintaining a thriving referral program.

And the great thing is that you probably already have the tools to rate your employees on the Alpha, Bravo, Charlie, Delta scale. Use performance review data and input from your managers and leaders to drive you toward the best candidates for quality referrals.

Since you're reading this book, I'd be willing to bet you and I share some similarities. You're in a position of management or leadership, you invest in your own education, and you're geared toward success. Odds are your best friend isn't lying on the couch right now playing video games or spending the entire weekend watching *The Real Housewives of Beverly Hills* three-day marathon. Think about your friends. Many of them are like you. The beauty of an employee referral program is that you can ask employees you really like for referrals.[3]

Tim Perkins, general manager at the Washington, DC, College H.U.N.K.S. Hauling Junk & Moving® flagship corporate location, probably said it best: "Most of the time great guys hang out with great guys. Knuckleheads hang out with knuckleheads."

---

3 Once again, please consult your state and local regulations regarding employee referral program disclosure.

Poaching: Realities and Opportunities

Poaching is when a company hires an employee from a competing company. Poaching can have a bad rap, particularly if it involves ignoring non-compete agreements, decimating a competitor's talent bench, or intentionally or inadvertently threatening relationships with partners and customers. (And yes, the term also describes hunting practices that are illegal.)

Corporate Responsibility Magazine reports that 92 percent of incumbent workers would consider jumping ship if a company with an excellent reputation offered them a job. The reality is that whether through an employee referral program or other recruiting means, you will end up hiring some of these incumbent workers away from another company—technically, poaching. The question is how to do so ethically and in a way that is consistent with the values that make you the best place to work in your industry and community.

I saw an example of poaching recently at a rest area off a local highway. A road paving crew stopped for some water and a break. The owner of another asphalt company approached the group and offered each person five dollars per hour more if they would quit on the spot and go work for him. As you might imagine, a number of those crew members dropped their shovels and orange vests and left right then and there.

You probably wouldn't think twice about poaching customers by offering them a better deal or discount, but when it comes to employees most business leaders and managers would do well to think twice before acting too impulsively. The question is this: In the cut-throat talent war, what constitutes ethical and good business practice?

Here are three poaching guidelines that will keep your legal status, reputation, and conscience intact.

1. Promote referral programs. Most HR experts agree that employee referral programs are ethical. A referral is, in essence, letting someone know about a job opportunity and letting an employer know of a potential candidate who happens to be employed currently by someone else. It's essentially information sharing. No commitments means no foul play.

2. Investigate non-competes. Non-compete agreements may or may not be enforceable depending on the state or location. Legal systems also are turning against the practice of using non-competes for many lower-skilled jobs, as the practice can be unduly restrictive. However, workers at all levels (and even interns) often sign non-competes. If non-competes are in play, you might want to consult a lawyer to make sure it's legal for a particular candidate to leave their job and work for you.

3. Work with ethical staffing agencies. Staffing agencies routinely approach incumbents for positions, which provides you with an extra layer of protection in the recruiting process. (We'll cover this subject more in a later chapter.)

Right about now, you may be asking yourself how you can prevent other companies and staffing agencies from poaching your employees. You know the answer—be a hunter in recruiting, engage your employees, and do your darnedest to retain those employees. Your best defense is being the best place to work.

Long-Term Rewards Incentivize Team Play

Let's say Samantha just referred Juwan, whom you have since hired. Should you give Samantha a bonus the day that Juwan starts? Or in six months? Maybe half now and half later to encourage Samantha to take Juwan under her wing to ensure her referral works out? What about giving Samantha a bonus on Juwan's hire-date anniversary as well? Because you hired her referral, something good happened. Always recognize and reward those things!

You might reward the longevity of both employees, the referrer and the referee—six months later, a year later, five years later. Give the new employee the day off on their hire-date anniversary. Or, so long as both parties are still with the company, allow them both to take the referred employee's anniversary off.

Longevity incentives offer many advantages and tend to boost loyalty and teamwork. The goal is to keep both Samantha and Juwan and reduce turnover. Any time your turnover decreases, your profitability increases. For example, if Juwan thinks he has found a better opportunity elsewhere, Samantha is incentivized to try to keep Juwan at the company longer and prevent him from leaving. Say a new manager doesn't know that Juwan always gets Wednesday nights off and keeps scheduling him for Wednesday nights. Samantha, the person who referred him, is going to be motivated to go to bat for Juwan because she's invested in keeping him around.

The Real Bottom Line

When you've built a great place to work and have created a knockout employee referral program, your biggest problem is going to be sorting through all the stellar applications. And remember—there's a big differ-ence between asking your employees to find a registered nurse versus someone to dig a hole. For a hard-to-fill position, one that requires a certification or advanced education, don't offer a small sundae at the local DQ. Instead, make the reward match the grind. Think about it this way: What would you pay an outsider if they were able to find you a solid performer, perhaps an Alpha- or a Bravo-level contributor? Now, what's an appropriate way to incentivize an employee of yours to go out and find that person and bring them to you?

Make the act of referring a friend, former colleague, or acquaintance worthwhile for your staff. If they're going to stick their necks out for you and encourage people they know and respect to apply, they need to be recognized with money, time off, a gift card—or all three. Acknowledge their effort in a way that turns them into a relentless recruiter of great talent for you.

When Russ Palmer bought Titan Restoration of Arizona in 2005, he had five employees. Today, Titan has more than 50 employees, and it's growing in size and revenue each year. "It all starts with hiring the right people," explains Russ. His office manager, Heather Biggs, has been with the company since 2010 and told me about Titan's top recruiting tactic: "Employee referral is our most successful recruiting program for new employees, and it also serves as a great retention tool for existing employees. Here's how ours works: The day a new employee starts, the employee who referred them to us receives a $500 check. If that new employee is still on the job six months later, the referrer receives an addi-tional $1,000 check. Now, if the employee is still with us two years after being hired, the person that brought them to us is rewarded with a pay-ment of $3,000." (WOW! $4,500 for getting your buddy to work at the same place you do! That might be a tad more inspiring than offering a $10 gift card to the local movie house.)

Consider mixing monetary with non-monetary incentives, such as offer-ing time off in addition to a cash bonus, giving the referring employee a public shout-out in a company-wide meeting, or recognizing the employee in a company newsletter. Get creative. Maybe you're trying to get a referral from an employee who wants to see her grandmother in Phoenix. It's off the wall, sure, but maybe, just maybe, she would bring you the candidate of your dreams if you offered to buy her two plane tickets to Phoenix. Bottom line: Make it worth your employees' time and energy.

First and foremost, you have to know your people. The Golden Rule goes like this: Do unto others as you would have them do unto you. However, serial entrepreneur Dave Kerpen offers this Platinum Rule instead: Do unto others as *they* would want done to them.

Don't make the mistake of assuming that everything's about money.

Food for thought—Jobvite's research indicates that

> **35 percent** of employees refer in order to help their friends
>
> **32 percent** refer to help their company
>
> **26 percent** refer in order to be viewed as a valuable colleague
>
> **only 6 percent refer for the money**[4]

To hire the best of the best, you need the help of your best employees. Give them what they want to get them to help you. Not sure what they want? Ask them.

Although many of my clients offer monetary bonuses for employee referrals, particularly if the referral remains on the payroll for at least 90 days, other smaller organizations may not have the discretionary funds available to pay such bonuses. As a result, many organizations have

4   Jobvite, "The Value of a Referral," *The Undercover Recruiter*, https://theundercover recruiter.com/infographic-employee-referrals-hire/.

developed creative alternatives to reward employees for committed referrals.

Take Miran Oca, for example. Miran runs Ocaquatics, a five-unit swim school located in Miami. She told me, "We have recruiting potluck parties, where team members invite friends they think would be a good addition to the team. We play Pictionary and other games. We've recruited a lot of great people at these parties. Watching people play Pictionary is the ultimate job interview!"

Reward the Effort, Not Just the Result

Too many employers say, "Refer someone, and if they're hired I'll give you a thank-you bonus." What happens if your employees refer someone who doesn't get hired? They spent effort recruiting and have nothing to show for it. In the end, a lack of reward discourages effort. Instead of offering a bonus only for hires, consider offering a bonus for any referral you get. The bonus doesn't have to be large. Maybe the employee gets a $5 Starbucks gift card, or for every referral brought in the employee gets to leave an extra 15 minutes early on the last Friday of the month. Reward the effort and not just the results, and you'll see referrals start pouring in.

Some might worry that such a reward system will lead to a flood of worthless referrals. It's possible but not likely—so long as your referral process is simultaneously simple and thoughtful. Consider putting a vetting process in place that requires the referrer to provide brief written answers to three questions:

I. How long have you known the candidate?

2. In what capacity do you know the candidate?

3. Why would the candidate make a strong, valuable hire for this company?

Then encourage employees to try and try again. You will land many of your best employees this way.

Tips and Tactics

In order to make employee referrals a high-yield tactic for your company, you first need to build a robust employee referral program. Follow these tips and tactics to optimize the number and quality of employee referrals you receive:

- Be a great place to work if you want your referral program to bring you real results.

- Help your employees understand what kinds of employees you're looking for by sharing clear, specific details about employee attributes, job qualifications, and job responsibilities.

- Train your employees on how to approach candidates. Make their jobs easy.

- Make employee referrals your top priority if you want to be FULLY STAFFED. Give employee referrals the VIP treatment.

- Know the ABCs of referral psychology, which is an essential element in maintaining a thriving referral program.

- Devise monetary and non-monetary rewards that encourage employee participation in your referral program. Reward employees who refer candidates who become successful new hires. In addition, offer incentives to all employees who take active steps to refer candidates for open positions.

Chapter 6

SAVVY MOBILE AND ONLINE RECRUITING STRATEGIES

I recently prepared for a first meeting with the manager of a small business. Naturally, I checked out the company online. I did a Google search and looked over their website. The site had a Careers page, which included a job posting dated a year earlier. I clicked on the job posting link and got an error message.

Next, I skimmed the company's social media pages. Near the top of the company's Facebook page was a photo of someone making an obscene gesture. A post on the page from a week earlier also included a negative comment about the company's founder.

At an opportune time during my meeting with the small business manager, I asked if he had seen the company's Careers page and Facebook page recently. "I didn't even know we had a Careers page or a Facebook page," was his reply.

If you lead or manage a business and don't know who's in charge of website and social media management and updates, you've got a problem. The best-case scenario: you're missing opportunities to communicate your brand identity to prospective candidates (and to prospective customers, for that matter). The worst case scenario: you're sending a terrible message to all who visit. You're basically saying either you don't know what's going on or you don't care.

Online and mobile recruiting strategies are vitally important when you want to be FULLY STAFFED. You can gain a digital resource that works silently in the background to actively promote your brand and job openings 24 x 7 x 365, has access to thousands of potential candidates, knows how to target the right new hires, and excels at facilitating candidate applications.

Online Recruiting Is Like Painting the Golden Gate Bridge

Construction on the Golden Gate Bridge started in 1933, and this magnificent structure officially opened for traffic in 1937.

Q: How long did it take to complete the painting on the bridge?

A: They've never stopped painting it. To protect the bridge from wind, corrosion, and the harsh sea air, a maintenance crew is always at work applying special high-tech paint where needed, and somewhere on the bridge it's always needed. Bridge painters will never get to the point where they put away their brushes and say, "Finally! We're done!"

You can expect something similar when it comes to your online recruiting strategies.

This book will certainly outlive the tactics that this chapter highlights. (The same holds true for all the chapters to follow.) Heck, by the time you read this, a lot of what follows might already have changed. However, the ideas behind these tactics are sustainable ones and are relevant at their core.

Small businesses are competing with big ones in the hunt for good talent. And big companies are competing with other big companies. It can be intimidating. Here's the key: regardless of the specific hiring tactics you use, the good news is that Internet and mobile recruiting can be powerful equalizers. Savvy Internet and mobile recruiting strategies can enable your business to hire great people and stay FULLY STAFFED without taking much time or breaking the bank. Here, I'll cover mobile recruiting tips that will get you on your way, including building user-friendly Careers and Jobs pages on your website, optimizing social media hunting strategies, and using online applicant tracking systems.[5]

It's All about the Candidate Experience

The right candidates are looking for the right jobs. They may be on an urgent fast track or a slow, exploratory journey. While they're searching for their next job, you want them to know you're hunting for candidates just like them. Here are the general phases of a candidate's mobile or online job search:

- **Phase 1: Discover** – The candidate finds you. (Many job seekers start with a Google search.)

- **Phase 2: Research** – The candidate reviews your company's website, LinkedIn page, Facebook page, and other online resources, as well as scans online information, such as job postings, looking for a good fit.

- **Phase 3: Apply** – The candidate applies and waits to hear from you.

---

5   The online world is dynamic and changing daily. I've tried to cover the basics in real time, but you'll need to do your homework to find the latest platforms and features that work best for your company's recruiting needs.

Each step of the way, the candidate has a positive or negative experience with your company. That means that a lot of what you're selling is an *emotional connection*, not necessarily a logical connection. Can candidates see themselves fitting in with the culture you're describing? Do they sense there's a friend in your company photos and videos? Is the work they're imagining a good fit for their strengths and interests?

Studies show that candidates who have a positive experience are more likely to refer others to you as a potential employer and are more likely to use your services and refer your services to others. The reverse is also true: if candidates have a negative experience, they're less likely to apply for a job or use or refer your professional services.

With those thoughts in mind, screen your company's digital reputation early and often. This advice bears repeating:

Screen your company's digital reputation early and often!

The Internet is an unforgiving archive. Your company's reputation is out there for anyone to find. All it takes is a simple search engine query— and *both prospective customers and prospective employees will be searching*. Have you looked at your company's digital imprint recently? Make it a regular practice. Start today and set your calendar alarm to do this at least once each month from now on.

Mobile Recruiting Tips

Not sure where the candidates are? Here's a hint: go mobile. As with in-person networking, the number one rule in this space is to *go where the candidates are*. When it comes to job hunting, candidates are using their phones and tablets all day, every day.

While nearly all job hunters in nearly all fields are mobile-centric, the Society for Human Resources Management (SHRM) says only 84 percent of employers use social media for recruiting and 66 percent are positioned for smart phone candidates. Given the societal shift toward mobile job hunting, many employers could use help climbing on board the smart phone train.

Mobile-friendly career page. Here's an easy test. Visit your company website from a mobile device. Is it easy to find, navigate, and access the Careers or Jobs page? Ask employees or others you trust to visit your page and share constructive feedback, and then make adjustments if necessary. (Depending on where you are in your mobile recruiting evolution, these adjustments may require some investment in mobile app design.)

Merging social media and mobile. Most LinkedIn and Facebook users access these platforms through their mobile devices. As with your website, make sure candidates can easily find and navigate your social media profiles and pages.

Mobile-friendly content. Videos that are easy to view are more likely to be shared than more traditional content. If you develop videos that promote your company or job openings, design them to be compatible with mobile and online platforms. Also allow applications to be completed and résumés to be forwarded through mobile.

Text messages. Have you ever been frustrated that you sent an e-mail to a candidate only to get a slow response? It may be that their preferred mode of communication is texting. Communicating by text offers several advantages. For example, research shows that text messages are read more than 95 percent of the time compared to e-mail messages, which are read only about 20 percent of the time. The best option is to be crystal clear about how you intend to communicate—or, if you're open to the idea, ask for a candidate's preference. Once you've established the rules, follow up by communicating throughout critical stages in the hiring process and, beyond that, when jobs open up in the future.

Also, strongly consider using a SMS text messaging service to make it super easy for interested job seekers to apply by texting an easy-to-remember and easy-to-spell word like "mason," "driver," or "apply" to a five-digit number, i.e., 54321, etc. These services, while not inexpensive, are remarkably effective in increasing your application flow as it's reported that more than 90 percent of all Americans have their mobile device within reach 24/7. You can find a service that works for you by entering "SMS text messaging service for recruiting" in your Web browser.

Website Recruiting—Maximizing Careers and Jobs Pages

When a candidate lands on your company's website looking for information about job openings, what will they find? I recently put myself in the mindset of a job hunter, and in a non-scientific experiment I visited ten websites of small(er) companies and independently owned franchise businesses that are looking for employees. Given what I found, I would be amazed to discover that any of these employers are having success with online recruiting.

In other words, here are the mistakes, problems, and blunders that almost every one of the companies I randomly chose are making in their digital recruiting:

Problem #1: *The Careers page is buried.* On the home pages of the ten companies, the first thing I looked for was a "Careers" or "Jobs" tab. Of the ten sites, this information was easy to find on only one page—that is, it was placed near the top of the home page. On three sites, there was no such page that I could find, and on six sites I had to scroll to find the Careers link in small print near the bottom of the page or click on "About Us" to find job-related information.

Solution: *Make your Careers or Jobs tab super easy to find, or even impossible to miss!*

Problem #2: *Use of generic or "stock" photos.* How do you feel about a company whose website features stock photos instead of real employees (as did nine of the sites I visited)? If you're like me, you'll probably feel uninspired by and disconnected from a company that uses generic images and will look elsewhere for one who proudly displays evidence of their great work culture and happy, engaged employees.

Solution: *Make a positive impression on candidates by showing real photos of real employees doing real work. Set yourself apart by being transparent and showing job seekers your people in action!*

Problem #3: *No context or story behind the title.* Several of the sites I visited listed job titles with no other information or description of what a specific job entailed. How is someone supposed to know what a *line cook* or a *form fabricator* does, what the requirements are for that job, and what kind of compensation and atmosphere people in that job can expect if they just see a job title?

Solution: *Make sure each job posting tells a story.* Give more than a job title; provide a thorough description of what each position entails; the specific education, experience, and skills that are required for that position; and what people who are hired in that position can expect. And don't just say, "competitive wages." This is your first chance to sell your culture and tell candidates what makes you a better employer than your competitors.

One site that stood out is College H.U.N.K.S. Hauling Junk & Moving®.[6] Started in 2005, College H.U.N.K.S.® now has 80 franchises across the United States and Canada. On their website, the "Jobs" tab is easy

---

6   H.U.N.K.S. stands for Honest Uniformed Nice Knowledgeable Service – https://www
    .collegehunkshaulingjunk.com/.

to find at the top of the home page. When you click on it, the first thing you see is a photo of actual employees smiling, followed by an invitation to learn more and possibly join the company.

The Jobs page also includes high-quality, compelling videos featuring actual frontline employees that tell the company's story and build on the company's commitment to their people, as well as videos of employee success stories and the company being featured on television shows such as MTV's *Jobs That Don't Suck*.

If I were looking for a job and encountered these messages, I'd be picturing myself standing with those guys in the videos and pictures and thinking: "This could be more than just a job. I could become part of a growing company with people who appear like they want to help me grow into more than just a mover. And they look like they're having some fun on the job and dress like a team. I'm in!"

The page also includes several "Apply" buttons and a chat feature. You'd have to be a complete idiot to not know how to proceed.

"Our secret sauce is definitely our team members," explains College H.U.N.K.S.® co-founder Omar Soliman. "What separates us from other moving and hauling companies is that we don't hire movers and haulers. We hire future doctors, future lawyers, future Fortune 500 executives. Our entire purpose and core value is building leaders." Talk about giving context and a compelling story behind what many might initially perceive to be an unsexy job.

But it doesn't end there. The College H.U.N.K.S.® recruiting page features a Benefits section that spells out nine compelling reasons an applicant would want to sign on: "great pay"; "dynamic culture"; "solid experience"; "great hours"; "bright future"; "stay fit and happy"; "we value diversity"; "work hard, play hard"; and "universal respect."

If you're a small business owner, you may not have the time or resources to build out a comprehensive series of Jobs pages like those on the College H.U.N.K.S.® site. With a little work, however, you can create a clear and inviting picture that helps candidates understand why they should work for you.

Social Media Recruiting

According to a recent SHRM survey, 84 percent of companies use social media in recruiting, while another 9 percent are planning to start using social media in their recruiting efforts. The big two social media platforms in the hiring arena are LinkedIn and Facebook. If you want to position your company effectively on them, you need to build a profile that is appealing and relatable to your target audience and then *create connections*. You'll want to include a summary about your company and regularly post current pictures and videos that reflect your culture and other information that would intrigue potential employees. Each platform also has distinct qualities and features, as I'll describe below.

LinkedIn Recruiting

LinkedIn is all business, all the time. More than 500 million professionals from around the world are members, and every day users develop their professional profiles, follow companies and individuals, and post billions of updates and messages.

Jason Sacco, managing partner of Critter Control, a successful brand franchise in the wildlife and pest control industry, has had success reaching candidates through LinkedIn. "Outside of employee referrals, I rely largely on LinkedIn as a resource," he says. "I use my knowledge of the industry to find qualified individuals who may not even be in the industry at all and entice them with the money, advancement, camaraderie, and transparency Critter Control offers. I have a high rate of recruitment through LinkedIn, and it also bolsters my employee referral pool when I headhunt qualified people on LinkedIn."

Below, I've included some tips for positioning your company for recruiting success on LinkedIn.

Create a company profile. Your company profile will likely be the first stop in your candidate's LinkedIn journey. It should include a slogan or headline about your company, a summary of the products or services you provide, and pictures and videos. Using searchable, job-specific phrases on your page will help candidates find you. For example, "health care aides" and "Washington state" are more specific than simply "health care." And if you and the other members of your management team don't already have personal profiles, create one, as job seekers will probably want to learn about you too.

Encourage employees to create profiles. Ask your employees to create LinkedIn pages that feature your company. While encouraging them to make their pages their own, you could provide sample text from the company profile, such as your mission statement and core values, that can help reinforce your brand and consistently communicate information about your corporate culture.

Develop your network. Your personal network consists of contacts who agree to connect with you. Your company will earn "followers" by participating actively and sharing content on LinkedIn. You can also invite contacts to connect through your company and personal pages.

Join LinkedIn Groups. In these virtual groups, members in the same business sector or with common interests can post and view jobs, network, and share information. For example, I searched recently for health care groups in LinkedIn and got 69 results. I found 22 groups in retail and 19 in transportation. You may want to find a few groups that are close matches and participate actively in those groups rather than joining too many groups and essentially not showing up.

Post jobs. You can post information about jobs for free on your company page or in groups, although you will get more visibility by posting paid job advertisements to reach candidates outside your network.

Search and contact candidates. Hiring managers and others can type a job title and geographic region in the search field (e.g., "truck driver" and "New Hampshire") and select "People." When a list of names pops up, you can invite them to connect (it encourages you to include an introduction or a personal message to increase the likelihood that your invitation will be accepted). Once connected, you can learn more about them from their profile. If you feel they might be a good fit, you can message them with a link to your job posting and share other relevant information. You can also contact members from groups you join and ask for referrals.

Post other information of value. You can publish posts to show you're an industry leader. For example, you could post that your company won an award, post to show support for Small Business Week or Manufacturing Month, share research about trends in your industry, or circulate a new professional survey that could be of interest to others. You can also "Like," "Comment" on, and "Share" posts.

Use the LinkedIn Talent Solutions paid service. LinkedIn has developed a suite of fee-based hiring tools called LinkedIn Talent Solutions that are designed to help with candidate searches.

LinkedIn Job Post Tips

When it comes to recruiting online, it's important to know the difference between a job posting and a job description. A *job description* starts as an internal document based on some form of job analysis that defines what it takes to do a job (objective, knowledge, skills), along with other qualifications. It usually includes information about the job such as salary and working conditions.

A *job posting* is designed to make the right candidate want to work for your company. While it should be consistent with information in the job description, it's generally shorter, crisper, and easier to skim.

Here are some tips for creating an enticing job posting:

- **Be succinct.** According to LinkedIn, the job posting generally should be shorter than a job description. An optimum length is 150–200 words.

- **Choose clarity over creativity.** A clear, descriptive job title is more search-friendly than a creative one.

(A job title such as Coffee Shop Server and Cashier is easier to find than Barista Extraordinaire.) Help candidates find you initially, and then incorporate creativity later in the job posting.

- **Be relatable.** Explain what the candidate needs to bring to the table—what you're looking for to support your needs and your culture (e.g., team player, adaptability, problem solver).

- **Explain your cultural pillars.** In addition to compensation and benefits, what is your company's commitment to helping employees grow and discover their potential? What are your values? What's the company atmosphere like? How much autonomy will the candidate have, and how does the company feel about communication and active listening?

- **Tell a powerful story.** Share videos, employee testimonials, and *real* pictures. Make it memorable (while also keeping it professional).

Facebook Recruiting

Facebook is the biggest social platform in the world, with more than 2.3 billion users and growing. You can promote your company's job opportunities on Facebook to try to reach the right candidates.

Companies like Two Men and a Truck have had great success hunting on Facebook. Tyler Whalen, a Two Men franchise owner, says, "Facebook has been a hotspot of recruitment for us of late. It's targeted, it's quick to fill out, and you can reach a wide audience. Facebook has been awesome in garnering interest from a younger crowd as well. The younger demographic is much more likely to respond to a Facebook notification than an e-mail. If they get that little red notification, they immediately want to follow up. Plus, they're likely to receive the notification on their phone, which they always have with them."

Kevin Cohen Plumbing in Eugene, Oregon, is very active on Facebook, consistently updating their page with posts and pics of employees and their families. Kevin knows that the outside world doesn't want to look at clogged drains, so he works to keep a fresh face on this hard, and often unsexy, work. His posts depict a vibrant workplace with tons of fun and interesting people who are doing fun and interesting things in their personal lives and also when they're out on the job. This has helped him build a brand in his community as THE place where great plumbers and HVAC techs work, making recruiting other skilled professionals much easier.

John DeFendis, a former world-champion bodybuilder and the founder and owner of Ultra Fit Personal Training in Greenville, South Carolina, is a huge believer in the recruiting power of Facebook. His page not only shows the "before and after" results that his signature programs achieve for the thousands of Ultra Fit clients, thereby attracting new customers, but it also works to pull in the best personal trainers from the Carolinas. "There are a ton of people who promote themselves as personal trainers," DeFendis told me. "But the percentage of those that actually understand the science of biology and physiology is embarrassingly small. My presence on Facebook has helped Ultra Fit attract the very best trainers from around the United States who want to become a part of a world-class training organization. When qualified trainers see the results our clients achieve and the culture our trainers enjoy, the applications and résumés pour in."

Below, I've included some tips for positioning your company for recruiting success on Facebook.

Create a Facebook company page. The goal is similar to LinkedIn—create a page that markets your company to potential job candidates. Facebook is definitely visual, so pictures and video go a long way.

Invite Facebook Friends. Hiring managers and others can build their network by inviting others to Like or Follow the company page. As with LinkedIn, you can use the Search feature and various filters to target likely candidates.

Post. Posts should focus on your company employees, work, and events in a positive, professional way. Here's how Two Men and a Truck positions itself on Facebook, according to Tyler Whalen: "Our Facebook posts consist of photos of our own guys and our own trucks, and we do a quick recap of what the company offers, such as what you can make hourly and benefits (paid time off, or PTO). We add catchy photos so that while you're scrolling through Facebook you might stop and read the message. We're able to boost our applications as well. Over the last weekend we got 14 applications. We triple our application count regularly through Facebook outreach."

Post jobs and job ads. You can post jobs in your company Facebook feed. You can also promote jobs through Facebook Referrals and Groups.

Find candidates. You can search for candidates based on such filters as job title, job sector, and geographic location. (For example, if you type "mechanic" and "Portland" in the search field in the upper left corner of the screen and then click on the "People" link, a number of profiles will appear.) You can research candidates further on LinkedIn or through a Google search. You can also invite people to Like or Follow your page and send them a message with your job posting or a link to it.

Run paid promotions. Facebook has paid promotion options for job ads as well.

Tyler Whalen explains that effective recruiting on Facebook is all about outreach. He says, "Our Facebook outreach involves more than posting. We go behind the scenes on Facebook and adjust the demographics that we're posting to. We cross-reference pages that people "Like" and post to like-minded individuals that way. Do we want an employee that's into hunting, fishing, and outdoors type of stuff? Then we'll target to those Likes. We also target certain zip codes. There are a bunch of different settings at your disposal on the back side of promoted Facebook ads. It's definitely not randomized when we post to Facebook. We're taking the data, analyzing it, and maximizing the return when we find a demographic or setting that is working. We're always asking ourselves, 'What worked, what didn't work, what can we do moving forward?'"

Recruiting on Other Popular Social Media Platforms

Other well-known websites can support your recruiting efforts. For example, you can tweet company and job information on **Twitter** and find candidates using clever hashtags. And you'd have to be living in a closet not to know about **Craigslist**'s classified advertising and its job board. Craigslist may charge fees based on your geographic area, but it's so well known among job seekers that it's foolish not to have your postings listed there.

Beyond traditional outreach, Scott Ramsey, area developer for the Office Pride Commercial Cleaning franchise in Tampa, uses Craigslist, Twitter, and other social media to alert the surrounding public about "open" interviews, which they hold at their office every Wednesday afternoon. Ramsey says these postings draw as many as 10–15 people at a time who come in for an interview and complete an application.

YouTube

Don't underestimate the power of video as a recruiting tool. Nothing will increase application flow more than having videos of your current employees telling others how much they love working for you circulating on the Net. No, not professionally produced "commercials" featuring paid actors, but rather authentic videos, maybe even recorded "selfie-style" featuring real people telling real stories about your workplace. Nothing is more convincing to a job seeker than watching an enthusiastic workplace review from actual employees.

Ginny Cameron, CEO of Cameron Insulation, based in Elkridge, Maryland, has experienced great hiring success with a video that showcases their company and its people. The video is posted on their website under a section called "Join Our Team," and includes testimonials from actual employees describing their experiences working for Cameron.

Big Job Boards

These sites compile and display jobs that are searchable by candidates. Some of the best known are Indeed, CareerBuilder, Glassdoor, Monster, and ZipRecuiter. The fees they charge vary. Here are two tips for using job boards:

- Post on more than one job board. You might post on one of the big ones and then on a couple of niche boards that are tied to your industry or the type of position you want to fill.

- Make sure the job boards you choose are mobile friendly.

Some niche job boards target different industry sectors and types of jobs. Here are a few examples:

- **Snag** (www.snagajob.com), an hourly online staffing platform very big with retail-, restaurant-, and service-sector jobs and extremely popular with teens and young adults.

- **Poached Jobs** (www.poachedjobs.com), a restaurant and hospitality staffing solution.

- **WorkInRetail** (www.workinretail.com), a retail job board.

- **ConstructionJobs** (www.constructionjobs.com), a construction and engineering job platform.

Another terrific resource to consider is **TraitSet®** (www.TraitSet.com). This is a comprehensive hiring tool that not only provides online application and onboarding help, but also features a behavioral assessment that can actually measure specific traits (e.g., honesty, reliability, etc.) to let you know how an individual is most likely to behave and perform for you before you make a hiring decision.

Online Tracking

Depending on the number of job openings, candidates, and other hiring tasks, a company may want to consider an online applicant tracking system (ATS). Employers can use an ATS as a central source for filtering candidate applications based on keywords, experience, skills, and more, as well as track where candidates are in the hiring funnel.

Here's how an ATS can work. Your team loads a job description into the ATS. The description populates to a job board that you specify, and you start receiving applications. You can include upfront questions as part of the hiring funnel, including "knock out" questions such as willingness to travel, handle shift work, or do manual labor. The ATS makes it easy to sort through applications, schedule interviews, and progress through the recruitment process.

A Few Words about EEOC Compliance

Whether or not you use applicant tracking software, it may be important for your company to track applicants.

Most businesses in the United States with 15 or more employees are legally required to meet the regulations enforced by the Equal Employment Opportunity Commission (EEOC). In 1978, the EEOC adopted the Uniform Guidelines on Employee Selection Procedures (UGESP). Employers should follow these procedures to ensure their selection processes are lawful and do not create disparate impact. For example, one best practice is for employers to track applicants based on demographic data to determine if a particular pre-hire assessment discriminates against members of legally protected classes at a higher rate than those of protected classes.

I'm not a lawyer, but I know that the EEOC takes discrimination in hiring seriously. (Trust me, it's a good thing.) If you're considering using an ATS or are capturing data on your candidates in another way, make sure that you're EEOC compliant.

Tips and Tactics

Candidates' experience with your company online can make or break their willingness to work for you. Follow these tips and tactics to optimize candidates' ability to find you, learn about you online, and apply for your open positions:

- Screen your company's online presence, including comments that are posted on your social media pages and other sites. Your online presence tells a story, positive or negative. Make sure you're the one guiding the direction of that story.

- Go BIG with mobile. Most job seekers (89 percent) say mobile devices are important when job searching—is your business positioned to optimize mobile?

- Make Careers or Job pages easy to find and navigate on your company website, and make their content clear and compelling for candidates.

- Maximize your use of LinkedIn, Facebook, and other social media platforms as part of your recruiting strategy.

- Consider making strategic use of an applicant tracking system (ATS), and make sure you comply with Equal Employment Opportunity Commission (EEOC) regulations.

Chapter 7

HUNTING AT JOB FAIRS
Where the Game Comes to You!

Shyla, a 17-year-old high school senior in Boise, Idaho, was eager to enter the workforce and was particularly interested in retail jobs. She heard about a job fair being held at her high school gym, a fair specifically targeted toward retail jobs in her community. She decided to attend, and she went all out: she researched the retailers scheduled to be there, wore a professional outfit, and brought copies of her updated résumé.

When Shyla arrived at the fair, she was taken aback. "Many employers were sitting at tables looking at their cell phones or talking to each other," she said. "Some just had a sign or banner on their table with some flyers and job applications, but that's it. The few people that I was able to talk to seemed like low-level employees who weren't prepared to answer questions about the company and often didn't even know what jobs were open. They just referred me to the company's online job portal. It was a total waste of time."

Let's just say that those employers made quite the (negative) first impression.

There are, of course, other and better ways to make a first impression. Case in point: Ariel was interested in a teaching position at a community college near her home in Baltimore. She has a degree in counseling and had been applying online for a job at the local college for several months without any reply. She read online that the college was going to participate in a local career fair, so she made plans to attend.

At the fair, Ariel introduced herself to the recruiter and said she had applied online but hadn't been contacted. The recruiter told her that the online system was blocking her because she had a counseling degree instead of an education degree. Nonetheless, as the recruiter further explained, Ariel was fully qualified for the position. Today, Ariel is now happily employed at the college as an instructor.

"If you hadn't come to this job fair," the recruiter told Ariel, "we wouldn't have had the opportunity to meet face to face, where I could discover that you're actually a great fit for us."

A Special Type of Hunting Opportunity

Job fairs, career fairs, and job expos are events where employers and recruiters get to meet with job seekers. Employers have the opportunity to introduce their company and open positions, and job seekers have the opportunity to meet directly with those doing the hiring. These fairs can be a tried and true way to reach a lot of potential employees.

If a career fair is part of your recruiting strategy, you need to be meticulous and thoughtful in your approach. Try to think about the fair from the job seekers' point of view. As Shyla's and Ariel's stories reveal, first impressions matter, and you surely don't want to invest time, money, and resources into a job fair only to have candidates write you off as a "total waste of time."

A job fair gives you a special type of hunting opportunity. It's one where your targets come to you. When digital recruiting fails to produce, job fairs can score big results. (Digital recruiting and job fairs can, of course, also work in harmony.)

To be clear, time, effort, resources, and strategic planning are required to make job fairs pay off. But when they do pay off—as you'll see in this chapter—YAHTZEE!

Types of Job Fairs

Before diving into the specifics of how to position your organization at a job fair, you need to decide where to invest your time and resources in this space. Most career fairs come with a price tag. The first step, then, is to choose the right ones for your company.

Community Job Fairs – These fairs may be sponsored by the local city or county government. Employers from a variety of industries gather in one location to meet prospective employees for jobs ranging from entry- to management-level positions.

Industry-Specific Job Fairs – These fairs focus on employers from a specific sector—health care, manufacturing, retail, trades, etc. Candidates tend to have experience or knowledge about the sector before they choose to attend the fair.

College/University Job Fairs – These events are held by local colleges, community colleges, and universities (generally on campus). They usually attract employers seeking candidates for entry-level positions that require a particular certification or degree.

Company-Specific Job Fairs – Some companies and chains hold their own job fairs (more on this later).

Virtual Job Fairs – Virtual fairs are online versions of traditional career fairs, and they're growing in popularity and creativity. At these online events, employers and job seekers meet in a virtual environment, using chat rooms, teleconferencing, webcasts, or e-mail to discuss job openings.

In May 2019, for example, an online initiative, National Youth Hiring Day, brought together employers, organizations serving youth, and high schools across the nation to connect young people between the ages of 16 and 24 who are out of school or unemployed with quality entry-level jobs. "Young people thrive when they have opportunity and the support they need to succeed," said Sheri Schultz, president of the Schultz Family Foundation, which promoted and provided financial support for the initiative. "National Youth Hiring Day is a way to expand our efforts to link businesses looking to attract and employ entry-level talent with young people who tend to face barriers to landing their first job."

A simple virtual application connected candidates with leading national companies (e.g., Enterprise Rent-A-Car, FedEx, Five Guys, Hilton, Hyatt, Macy's, Nordstrom, Starbucks, T-Mobile, Target, and Ulta Beauty). Job seekers also had the opportunity to attend face-to-face job fairs and training events held at high schools in 16 states.

Job Fair Hunting Tactics

Let's say you've chosen a job fair that's a good match for your company. You plan to set up a booth in a room full of people who need jobs, a room filled with competitors' booths. How can you attract the diamonds in the rough and ensure that you're getting the best fit?

Below are ten tactics—some conventional, some less conventional—you can use to increase the odds that you'll find strong candidates for your open positions at your next job fair.

1. Plan for success. Don't be fooled into thinking that job fairs are just about bringing a logoed table banner, rounding up some flyers, printing a sign-up sheet, sending HR reps to the gym, and setting out a bowl of lollipops to attract students. As with any initiative, getting the most out of a job fair requires creative thinking and business-minded planning. You'll need the right decision-makers at your company to support your goals. Do you want to hire on the spot, collect applications and/or résumés, or simply build your brand? How does the career fair fit into your overall hiring strategy? How will you determine ROI?

Once you've done the upfront work, consider which job fairs make the most sense. Look around at least a couple of months in advance to take advantage of early registration discounts. Once you sign up, you can then begin to tackle the details about who should attend, which promotional materials you should invest in, and what the timelines should be. Your promotional strategy (more on that below) and budget should also be on the planning list. Also, be sure to determine accountability for each stage of execution before, during, and after the event.

2. Get the word out! What good would a career fair booth be if nobody showed up? You'd be wasting your company's investment and your marketing employees' time if they burned a day with nothing to show for it. If you're participating in a career fair, use your connections and media contacts to GET THE WORD OUT in advance.

Promote your attendance on social media sites like Facebook and LinkedIn. Run an Indeed or other career site ad promoting your participation. Print flyers announcing that you'll be interviewing and hiring prospective employees at the fair, and post those flyers on community boards and at local grocery stores, churches, and colleges. Capture the attention of the people you want to hire, along with the attention of their friends, significant others, and family members who can spread the word. Never underestimate word of mouth. High visibility is guaranteed to improve your chances of meeting your future superstar at a job fair.

And make sure your flyer and social media posts share compelling information about why someone would love to work for your company (WIIFM), describe open positions, and include engaging pictures that reflect your culture.

3. Send the right company representative. Sending HR and marketing reps to a career fair is a good start, but it's not enough. Sure, HR will be able to handle questions about benefits, pay, and time off, and your marketing rep will be able to spout off the company manifesto and five-year vision for the future. But if you also send someone who intimately understands the job that you're hiring for, then you'll be ahead of the game. For example, if your goal is to fill the position of line cook, send the kitchen manager.

When you send the direct supervisor for the open position to the job fair, you're banking on the fact that they will know their ideal team dynamics, and you're also giving potential hires insight into what "real" employees look like at your organization. Bonus: you're also showing the supervisor that you trust them to make the right choices for their team. All of these factors play to your benefit in finding the right person for a job.

Candidates' interest is further piqued when they can talk to someone who is actually *doing* the same job they're applying for. What's a typical day like? What work will they actually be doing? What are the pros and cons of the job? Who better to answer these questions than someone who is happily engaged in their present position—this is where the rubber meets the road, folks!

Be sure to coach your representatives about their important role in the fair. They should be standing in front of the display, not lounging behind the table. Their body language should be open and welcoming, and they should smile at and make eye contact with those passing by. They should be prepared to engage with those who show even the slightest bit of interest by inviting them to participate in some sort of non-threatening activity (e.g., a construction company might invite attendees to see how many swings they need to hammer a nail flush into a 2 x 4). Above all, your representative should know how to talk to anyone who might look like a potential candidate.

4. Interview and hire on the spot. Depending on the position you're hiring for, it may be a wise and competitive move to empower the direct supervisor, HR rep, or hiring manager to hold interviews or even hire people on the spot at a career fair. The talent war is being waged on all fronts, so if an all-star approaches, by all means don't let them walk away. You've got a room full of hungry job seekers. Give yourself the best chance at hiring them, or someone else will be waiting in the wings to snatch them up.

At the very least, give your team the authority to schedule in-office interviews as soon as possible. If you want to be fast on the trigger, you'll need to decide in advance how you can streamline and expedite the hiring process to your ultimate advantage.

5. Make a dynamic, eye-catching display. When you want to stand out in a cattle call environment, you need to understand that everyone in the room will be vying for the attention of the superstars who walk by. It takes a lot more than a sign-up sheet and a bowl of candy to entice people to swing by your booth or talk to you.

You don't need a ring toss or a dunking booth to engage your prospects, but you should be thinking outside the box! Remember the construction company example above? I recently went to a high school job fair where medical office staff showed attendees how to take their friend's blood pressure and check their heart rate using sophisticated equipment. At that same fair, the local auto dealership, desperately seeking auto techs, let students put computer chips in a "Fast and Furious"-type car to see the change in horsepower.

If you run a pest control service, set a taxidermy opossum front and center on your table. If you own an audiovisual company, project cool video imagery onto the back wall or set up a wireless microphone to attract employees like a moth to a flame. Not sure what your company should do? Display a large-scale visual of the career trajectory of an employee (again—WIIFM). You get the idea.

The point is this: Go above and beyond. Be interesting. Be weird. The more you have to talk about at your booth, the more people you're going to attract—and that's what job fairs are really about. Presenting yourself in unprecedented ways will not only get the attention of the people you want to hire; it will also get a crowd of people around your booth wondering what's up with that opossum.

6. Bring materials to distribute. If ten people are waiting in line to talk to someone at your extremely interesting booth, it makes sense to have materials with all the FAQs outlined so that their conversations with your representatives can be as meaningful as possible. Your HR rep will gladly say that you offer full benefits, but if they have supporting materials to distribute—videos, pamphlets, on-the-job photos, employee testimonials, career path maps, and lists of specific benefits—then you're playing a much more effective game.

Most people you'll end up talking to at the fair will have little to no idea what your company does or why your company is great. Providing them with real information—beyond the job title and description—will go a long way toward making sure that the people who stick around are worth your time. If a candidate actually reads the ten employee testimonials you've compiled, you may have a potential hire on your hands who not only wants to work for you but also respects your transparency and understands how your business is different from the other businesses in the room.

7. Arrive early and build win-win relationships. Arrive very early so you can claim the best spot in the room, as well as start networking and relationship-building before candidates even get there. Meet as many people as you can, introduce your business, and learn what you can about theirs.

Not only are you setting an example that yours is the kind of company that goes out of its way to support others and think about the big picture, but suddenly everyone in the room knows what you're doing there. Everyone can recruit for you. If someone at an IT booth is interested in private security instead, the IT booth recruiters know exactly where to point them. You're providing value by playing matchmaker for other companies, and you've multiplied the matchmaking capacity for your jobs.

I can't say enough about this simple yet highly effective idea. With so many different employment options in one room, you can increase the odds of connecting with the right people by being a great communicator, giving without expectation of return, and going above and beyond to showcase the kind of energy, commitment, and work ethic your company both demands and inspires.

Just as there are many advantages to being the first one in the room (having your pick of table location is just one), there are benefits to being one of the last ones to leave (don't leave early!). Show prospective employees that you take this hiring process seriously, and they'll take note.

Seth Ryan is the HR Director at a branch of Signal 88, a private security franchise. He attends his share of career fairs. His secret to success is being the first one in the building.

"When I go to a job fair," Seth says, "I show up as soon as the doors open so I'm one of the first ones in the room. I help the staff set up the tables and get ready for the event, and I get the pick of positions in the room. From my prime position, I greet everyone as they come in, whether they're looking for Signal 88 or not.

"I've also already gone around the room and asked other recruiters if they need help setting up their booths before we start as well. When I ask others if they need help setting up their booths, they assume that I work there. When I tell them about Signal 88, they're always surprised to find out that I'm running a booth like them. I'm networking. I'm learning what all these other companies are doing so that when someone comes in looking for manufacturing or IT or whatever I know who to send them to.

"It sets a precedent that Signal 88 has a good name through networking and through working to understand people's needs."

Wow! Seth really understands the value of personal connections. Fantastic tip!

8. Recruit—it's why you're there! I've been to trade school fairs, job fairs at high schools, career fairs at hotel ballrooms, and every kind of fair in between. I always see the same things: people milling about, unsure of where they should go or what to expect. Frankly, things can get awkward when you're first exchanging introductions. It can feel like a blind date. Everyone knows *why* they're there, but sometimes initiating a conversation can be difficult.

With some exceptions, people aren't going to stroll up, introduce themselves, and put in an application. You're going to need to do a lot of the heavy lifting. If you're going to head into the woods, you need to hunt. Don't sit around waiting for the game to wander over.

Making the first move is often the right move. You don't have to grab passersby by the collar or yell at them as they pass. Instead, be personable. Exude confidence. You may be surprised how far a little bravado can go. Greet people by the name on their nametag and ask if they'd like to know more about what you do. Don't be put off if half or more say no. Your goals are to engage and recruit the right people, and being friendly and proactive will help you achieve those goals.

9. Compile candidate information (that's part of the ROI). During the planning process for a job fair, consider how you define success. If you don't know how many interviews you've held or how many employees you've gained through fairs, then you also may not know whether or not the fairs are worth your company's time.

Carrie Corbin, former global head of talent attraction, employer brand, and diversity recruiting at American Airlines, says it's hard to track ROI from career fairs. "You're also standing there herding cats with a bunch of other companies," she says. "It can be a nightmare to keep track of everyone."

Using a customer relationship management (CRM) system the same way you would with your customers can help solve this problem—and it offers other benefits as well. When customers come through the checkout line at a retail clothing store, the clerk asks for their phone number or e-mail address to begin the CRM process. Customers have to be part of a store's reward program to get grocery discounts or coupons. In exchange, the store gets customers' personal information. Capture the same kinds of information from people interested in working for you.

Developing a CRM-style database for career fairs and other outreach helps companies improve recruiting databases and stay connected to prospects. As with all aspects of hunting, make it easy on candidates—it should take no more than a minute or two to collect candidate information.

Having candidate information at your fingertips after a career fair can be invaluable even after you hire for a specific position. Think about it—you've just given yourself a pool of possible candidates the next time a similar position opens at your company. Taking information from everyone who stops by your booth makes it possible to track engagement rates while also building up your back stock of future recruits. That sounds like successful hunting to me.

10. Hold your own career fair. Why not put the ball in your own court by hosting your own career fair? I recently discussed this idea with Lea Bell, a recruiter and organizer at SiteWise, a gas and utility installation and maintenance company headquartered in Wheat Ridge, Colorado.

With just over 400 employees, SiteWise is by no means a large company. Nonetheless, they started hosting their own in-house career fairs in 2017. Lea told me that their HR team came up with the idea and convinced managers from each department to host different sections of the fair.

"We represent our departments at different tables," she says. "We have managers posted at each table so each can talk about their department. We bring in trucks and equipment and demonstrated the things we do like fusing gas pipes and digging ditches.

"Usually about fifty or so candidates turn out for hiring events, which has led to about twenty hires. We promote the events on social media and Craigslist and contact people who've sent us résumés. I send out reminders to my contacts through job fairs and trade schools to generate interest. We have one or two three-hour fairs each year. All of these hiring events have been successful."

Did you catch that math? Fifty potential candidates at each event, twenty hires from each event, and all in three hours. That's crazy! (Of course, that doesn't include time for planning and follow-up, but I'd still call that efficient recruiting.) Holding your own career fair is a great idea, especially if you have a ton of roles to fill for a busy season or if you're looking to expand your workforce quickly.

Most importantly, they had a captive audience. Every single person in the building was there to learn about job opportunities at SiteWise. They didn't have to compete with other companies for attention, and they were ready to hire on the spot. Lea used her existing network to build interest and get the word out, and then she delivered.

When she was in charge of recruiting delivery drivers for three major Anheuser-Busch distributors in Oklahoma, Carrie Corbin realized that her executive team had all been promoted up from "Bud Guy" truck drivers. She discovered that they thought this was a sexy job and they liked recruiting for these positions as if it was, in fact, a sexy job. That led to an oversaturation of misinformed applicants who didn't work out.

So Corbin persuaded Budweiser to promote their own job fair rather than attend executive job fairs, where their booths recruiting route drivers were positioned between companies that were recruiting for more glamorous jobs for brands like Google and Disney. The career fairs she put on were held at the Budweiser centers and drew people who were highly interested in working for Anheuser-Busch. Corbin empowered her hiring managers to make job offers on the spot as long as they properly vetted the candidates. "It was the first time in the history of those Budweiser branches that we filled all these jobs at 100 percent capacity," Carrie told me.

Consider organizing something similar for your own business. Build some presentations, get managers from different departments on board, spread the word, and host your own career fair. You may be surprised at how efficient it can be when every person in the room is there to learn more about your company or possibly work for you.

Tips and Tactics

Here's a checklist you can use before, during, and after your next job or career fair:

Before the Job Fair

- ❏ Hold a strategic planning meeting with the right decision-makers.
  - ❏ Align on the value of a career fair. Determine how fairs fit in with the company's overall hiring strategy, and document your goals.
  - ❏ Decide which career fairs can best help you reach your objectives.
  - ❏ Pinpoint your budget.
  - ❏ Decide who should be involved in designing and executing the tactics to make the fair a success.
  - ❏ Make policy decisions (e.g., decide if reps can interview and hire candidates on the spot).
  - ❏ Decide how you will measure ROI and success.
- ❏ Register for the career fair—and do it early enough to take advantage of any early-registration discounts.
- ❏ Hold a tactical planning meeting with your management team.
  - ❏ Create a planning timeline, and determine individual roles and responsibilities.

- ❑ Determine who from the company should attend the fair.
- ❑ Document travel and logistical needs (e.g., transportation, lodging, materials shipment, name tags).
- ❑ Nail down your strategy for collecting candidate information at the fair (e.g., CRM).
- ❑ Hold a promotions and outreach meeting with the right team members.
  - ❑ Align on your outreach strategy. Will you use online ads? Social media? Flyers?
  - ❑ Create a planning timeline, and determine individual roles and responsibilities.
  - ❑ Determine what information your promotional materials should include. (Don't bury the lead—identify the most compelling, differentiating message you'll use when hunting.)
  - ❑ Decide what materials you'll distribute (e.g., brochures, giveaways, business cards).
  - ❑ Create a plan for designing signage and building a dynamite booth display.
  - ❑ Create an internal communications plan (e.g., decide how employees might help to promote your participation in the fair).
- ❑ Hold a meeting with company reps to align on logistics.
  - ❑ Make travel and hotel reservations.
  - ❑ Transport materials to the location.
  - ❑ Decide how you'll set up and tear down the booth.
  - ❑ Determine booth and candidate interaction protocols. For example, should reps eat at the booth? Use their phones? When should they take breaks? How

should they approach candidates, collect candidate information, and handle résumés?

During the Job Fair

- ❏ Arrive early to set up and network.
- ❏ Ensure reps are actively involved in recruiting during the fair based on the strategies agreed to in planning sessions (e.g., engaging candidates using positive eye contact and body language, asking questions, not preoccupied with phones).
- ❏ Ensure reps track candidate information as agreed upon during the planning sessions (e.g., simple sign-in sheet monitored by designated rep, collecting business cards).
- ❏ Stay late (or at least don't leave early)!
- ❏ Break down the booth and ship materials.
- ❏ Take care of any open bills and accounts.

After the Job Fair

- ❏ Follow up promptly with candidates based on the timeline established in the planning meeting.
- ❏ Capture and document success metrics.
- ❏ Hold one or more debriefing meetings to identify strategies and tactics that worked and ideas for continuous improvements over time (e.g., What was the return on investment in terms of finances and time of staff members? Were there any direct hires from the fair? Will there be any indirect hires or other benefits based on building brand awareness and/or referrals? How did this fair compare to others? Would the company benefit from attending this or similar fairs in the future?).

Chapter 8

STAFFING AGENCIES
As Workforce Optimization Partners

In a manufacturing plant outside of town, temporary and contract employees work with teams of full-time skilled machinists to complete a massive order that will keep a major client from changing to an overseas vendor.

At the convention center hotel downtown, a large crew of temporary workers is cleaning up after a week-long trade show, making certain they ready the property for the giant auto expo booths that will be set up the next day.

An experienced truck driver just made an urgent delivery to the local hospital. He lives two states away, but a staffing agency brought him to town and put him up in an extended-stay motel as part of an effort to help a large metropolitan area recover after a devastating storm.

Companies and organizations of all shapes and sizes are depending more and more on staffing agencies to help them ease their labor challenges in these tumultuous times. According to the American Staffing Association (ASA), more than three million temporary employees are on the job during an average week in the United States. Along those lines, roughly 15 million people accept flexible work assignments each year.

Does your business:

- Have a high demand for seasonal work?

- Perform production or service work that fluctuates radically based on customer demand?

- Need fill-in labor when full-time staff go on leave?

- Take on labor-intensive short-term projects like facility moves, new product launches, or holiday blowout sales?

- Want to assess employees' potential before hiring those employees full time?

If so, temporary and contract workers could provide the cure for your workforce blues.

You can always hire temporary workers directly, meaning that you recruit them and take responsibility for salaries, benefits, background checks, and other legalities. However, if you aren't inclined to take on this level of hiring effort (and the truth is that temp hiring does take some work), you might choose to hire temporary workers through a staffing agency that will work with you to assess the best options for your business and send qualified workers your way.

While you'll pay a mark-up on employees you find through a staffing agency, the time and hassle you save could very well be worth the additional cost.

The Origin and Rise of Temp Agencies

Staffing agencies today provide comprehensive employment services to organizations of all sizes in all sectors. Of course, the staffing agency (or temporary/recruiting agency) model has evolved over time. The origin of staffing agencies in the United States goes back to the 1940s. When soldiers enlisted to defend our country in World War II, they left companies struggling to fill the jobs they left behind. Housewives were recruited to fill the void, many of them as part-time workers. After the war, our soldiers returned to assume new positions, and the market for finding temporary workers evolved into a profitable industry. Founded in 1946, Russell Kelly Office Service (now called Kelly Services) became the link between Kelly Girls (women who could handle the office work) and the companies desperate to hire workers.

While companies have used temporary workers since the 1940s, labor economists point to the Great Recession of 2007–2009 as a period when outsourced staffing increased as a viable workforce strategy. After companies laid off workers, they analyzed future employment needs in a radically different way. Rather than hiring full-time staff in good times only to lay them off during bad times, many companies started hiring temporary employees to serve as a labor force buffer, or put another way, a "cushion."

Today, hiring temporary and contract employees is an integral part of the staffing strategy for a wide range of companies and organizations in every industry and market sector. Temporary agencies can help you fill jobs and positions of every possible type and level, which means you can now find a contract CEO almost as easily as a contract custodian. The best part? When temporary employment is handled correctly, every party in the transaction wins.

ASA president and chief executive officer Richard Wahlquist, an industry thought leader, explains that even with all the technology and advancements in staffing it still comes down to the human element. "The basics have not changed even with fancy technology in the recruiting space," he says. "You need to establish yourself as the best place to work. Then you need to know who needs to be on your bus and in which seat and then communicate that information in terms that candidates can understand.

"It's like dating. You meet a wonderful person but want to spend some time getting to know them before buying a house and moving in together. Staffing agencies can take the risk out of hiring and help create a win-win situation for your business and employees."

Wahlquist also underscores the value that today's staffing agencies can provide to small businesses that may not have a full HR department or may not have an HR department at all. "Recruitment process outsourcing is when a staffing agency outsources part or all of its recruiting function to an outside agency," he says. "This outsourcing can include sourcing, recruiting, interviewing, onboarding, and more." Agency employees can work virtually or work onsite at the client's place of business on a project-based (generally three- to six-months) or longer-term engagement.

Why Staffing Agencies Might Be Your Ideal Workforce Partner

Below, I'll share five reasons why you should consider hiring temporary and contract employees through a staffing agency.

1. Let the agency do the heavy lifting for you. Recruiting and hiring can be expensive and time consuming. When you channel the resources of a qualified staffing agency, you won't have to spend time sifting through résumés, interviewing candidates, and negotiating employment terms. Staffing agencies are experts in all aspects of the employee life cycle and will do the heavy lifting for you so you can focus on your core business.

Of course, their services come at a price. Depending on the positions you're looking to fill, the agency will forward a few top candidates or just the one they believe to be the best fit for the work you need done. And if you need lots of people—and you need them fast—the agency route may be your best option.

2. Find qualified workers much faster. Have you ever needed more workers to get a job done...and you needed those workers yesterday? Let's say you have the opportunity to close a huge sale that will dramatically increase your business. YAHOO! But wait, this business increase means you'll need to ramp up production. Clearly, it'll be a lot more work than your existing staff can handle.

Do you accept the sale or pass it on to a competitor? Decide fast... the clock is ticking.

Odds are that an industry-specific staffing agency has a network of people in place to answer your quick-turnaround needs. Choose a staffing agency willing to establish a strong working relationship with you. If possible, find one that has expertise in your industry or business sector.

Wahlquist explains the full range of services offered by today's organizations. "They certainly can take orders," he says. "However, most recognize that the best result comes when they understand your business and your strategy. They will ask questions to understand the jobs you need to fill and the technical skills necessary. They'll also seek to understand your culture so they can send you the best possible people. Many agencies also offer training for temporary candidates to help ensure your specific needs are met."

Staffing employees work in a variety of industries. The chart on the next page shows the percentage of temporary and contract employees in several industry sectors in the United States.

Industry	Percentage of Flexible Workers	Average Assignment Length	Examples of Jobs
Industrial	37%	14 weeks	Transportation and construction jobs, food handlers, assemblers, maintenance workers
Office, Clerical, & Administrative	28%	15 weeks	Receptionists, data entry, cashiers, call center reps
Professional & Managerial	13%	19 weeks	Accountants, attorneys, advertising & marketing
Engineering, Information Technology, Scientific	13%	23 weeks	Computer programmers, mathematicians, lab technicians, architects
Health Care	9%	15 weeks	Physicians, nurses, dentists

Source: American Staffing Association

3. Save time and resources. While temporary employees work at your place of business, they aren't *your* employees; instead, they're actually employed by the staffing agency. That means the agency, as your vendor, is responsible for paying their wages, providing any employee benefits, and making certain all related taxes and insurance programs (e.g., Social Security, workers' comp, and unemployment) are paid and recorded.

The way the agency makes their money is by charging you, the client company, a fee in terms of marking up the employee's hourly wage. To determine if a mark-up is worth it, compare the agency's hourly rate against all the costs involved in recruiting and hiring, payroll and benefits (including vacation, sick pay, and possibly health insurance), training and development (if applicable), and employee turnover.

You may find that you'll save time and resources that would otherwise bog down your HR and payroll staff. Do the math, and you might even discover that the hourly rate you're billed from the agency is a bargain!

4. Improve the morale of your current workforce. Employees who are overworked and pressured to produce more in less time can easily become tired and resentful—and they may even be at increased risk of health and safety issues. They also tend to be less productive and more inclined to seek out a new position elsewhere. In other words, your overall workplace culture will suffer.

That's why many existing workers see temporary and contract additions to the team as a good thing. As the saying goes, "Many hands make for light work!" When well-chosen temporary employees are brought in to lighten the staff workload, morale improves, along with productivity.

5. Try before you buy. "Temp-to-hire" is when a staffer is brought into a company on a temporary basis with the potential of becoming a full-time employee. The benefit to you is that the temporary employment serves as a probationary period—or a "dating" period, as Wahlquist refers to it. Because the employee is paid through an agency, you aren't responsible for benefits and other employment costs. The temporary worker remains an employee of the staffing agency during this time, so if you don't offer the temp worker a full-time position, you don't need to pay unemployment insurance or severance.

A key benefit here is that the temporary period gives you time to assess the staffer's performance in real-world conditions to determine if there's a good fit. Another benefit is that your business has the time to ride out any economic fluctuations that may impact the need for additional employees.

If your company decides to hire a temporary or contract worker in a full-time capacity, you'll pay a finder's fee to the agency. While paying a fee may not seem ideal, you'll gain a clear advantage in trying before buying so you can increase the odds that you land the right employee.

Finding the Right Staffing Agency for Your Business

You have thousands of staffing agencies and hundreds of different types and kinds of agencies from which to choose. Overwhelming, right? Ultimately, you'll want to narrow the list down to one or two that clearly match your business needs. As with any vendor you work with, you should invest time and effort into finding the one that's right for you.

You can start by asking for referrals from businesses you respect, perhaps current vendor partners. Learn about their experiences in hiring temporary workers, and be sure to check references from third-party sites, previous clients, and organizations like the Better Business Bureau and your local chamber of commerce.

You can also do a simple Google search (e.g., staffing agency, manufacturing, Ohio). As one example, the ASA database is searchable by location, company name, and job function (e.g., direct placement, temporary help, temporary to hire, long-term and contract help, recruitment process outsourcing). The agencies included in the database have earned the **Safety Standard of Excellence** from the ASA and the

National Safety Council. The mark signifies that a staffing firm is committed to the safety and well-being of temporary workers by complying with related requirements and demonstrating best practices.

The important thing here is to do your homework.

During initial conversations with an agency, be prepared to describe the types of workers you're looking for (by job title as well as skill set, experience level, and culture fit), the number of workers you need, and your projected timeline. You'll want to ask detailed questions about the agency's selection and candidate screening process, the benefits they provide (do they carry workers' comp, for example), and any temp worker training they provide. Specific contracts and procedures will vary by agency, so dig deep.

Bringing Temporary and Contract Workers on Board

Before introducing temporary workers into your workplace, your management team should think through the implications of integrating them into your existing teams. Are you looking for a temporary/contract hire or a temp-to-hire? If it's a true temporary position, how long is the anticipated employment period? What if you want to decrease or increase that employment period? If it's a temp-to-hire position, how and when will you (and the agency) evaluate performance, and in what ways will you use that performance data in making a hiring or release decision?

Remember when I said that hiring temporary employees can be good for morale and your corporate culture? Well, if your decisions aren't communicated properly, hiring temp workers can lead to trouble. Full-timers caught off guard by the new kids on the block may fear that their jobs are in jeopardy once they see their "replacements" arrive. Poor communication can create an "us vs. them" scenario, and it can get ugly. You can't afford that.

Clear, open communication with your existing staff is critical.

Great leaders, managers, and cultures always put solid policies and procedures in place before bringing temporary workers on board. They also always explain to their existing staff why they're bringing on additional help and how those workers will fit in with the culture and current work processes and schedules.

Here's a simple example of language a manager could use at a weekly staff meeting: "As you know, we have a big push through the end of the holiday season. To make everyone's lives more manageable, we're bringing on two temporary workers through the end of December. They'll join us on the floor starting next Monday. I hope you'll make them feel welcome!"

Encourage your permanent staffers to greet temporary employees warmly and to treat them with respect, not as short time fill-ins. Find a way to reward permanent staffers who go out of their way to welcome and mentor new temp workers. These staffers can model behaviors that will help new people quickly adapt to your culture. Really, these staffers are essential to your company's ongoing cohesion and productivity.

Along those lines, make sure you set up each and every one of your temporary and contract employees for success while reducing their risk of failure. If you onboard your permanent hires (and you should), simply extend that same practice to temp employees.

Most staffing agencies will want to be part of that onboarding process and will inform employees what they should expect before the first day of an assignment. It's not unusual for a staffing agency representative to visit the workplace in advance to get a good sense of the physical and cultural environment so they can tell temporary employees what to expect before day one. All of these initial steps work in your favor. After all, you want temporary employees to be motivated, engaged, and fully present. Don't cut corners.

Western Water Works' Temp Strategy Leads to Loyal, Long-Term Employees

Located in Southern California, Western Water Works (WWW) supplies water pipes and fittings to large companies and communities all over the Southwest. One element of their success has been hiring temporary and contract employees, watching how they perform during their probationary period, and setting those temporary workers up for long-term success at the company.

WWW's comprehensive workforce strategy is focused on hiring temporary workers as the first stage in its STEPS program. Through the STEPS program, new temporary employees discover what they would actually be doing if they were hired full time. The program features six levels of employment, and hundreds of employees have followed an amazing path from temporary positions to higher-level jobs that best suit their skills and interests.

Here are the six levels, from bottom to top:

1. Temporary Employee
2. Driver/Material Handler
3. Assistant Supervisor
4. Supervisor
5. Account Manager
6. Director of Sales

"The STEPS program has been key to the company's growth and expansion," says WWW president Bruce Himes. "Each step has a knowledge and skills checklist that must be completed and verified to step up to the next level."

Brad Peterson, a WWW account manager, says that starting as a temporary worker at Western Water Works strengthened his long-term loyalty to the company. "After researching the company, I saw the opportunity that was available at WWW," he notes. "I drove as a temp driver for two months, and in that time I learned how things are done at WWW. I was instantly impressed with how the company pushed to train and make all of their people better. From the operations checklists, the sales checklists, and the training throughout, WWW has set me up for success since the day I started as a temp. They saw what I could do, and I got to learn what this amazing company is all about!

"Working for a company that believes in its people and has a clear-cut vision is wonderful," Brad continues. "My career with them may just be starting, but my plan is to make a lifetime career out of this incredible opportunity."

Tips and Tactics

- Do your homework to find one or more staffing agencies that are right for your organization. Today, staffing agencies offer a full range of HR support, from referring temporary and contract workers to serving as full-service HR partners. Some firms specialize in virtually every sector, while others specialize in your sector and your needs.

- Calculate the value of partnering with a staffing agency in terms of the investment you'll make in sourcing, recruiting, interviewing, hiring, and performing other workforce functions.

- Determine who at the company should be involved with the agency. If you're recruiting temporary or contract workers, it makes sense to include the department head where they will be working. For longer-term strategic engagements, company leaders may want to be involved.

- Be prepared to answer staffing agency questions about your short- and long-term workforce optimization needs and to ask questions about the agency's services and offerings.

- Determine onboarding roles and responsibilities between your company and the staffing agency. Then onboard your temporary and contract employees just as you would your permanent employees.

- Communicate to your permanent employees any plans to bring on temporary workers. Engage them in the process, and you may well boost morale.

Chapter 9

COMMUNITY NETWORKING
Transforming Contacts into Connectors

There was a popular TV commercial that ran in the 80s for Fabergé Organics shampoo. The lovely pin-up model and actress Heather Locklear said that this shampoo was so good that "I told two friends about it, and they told two friends, and those friends told two friends, and so on, and so on…"

Fabergé's point? The planting of just two seeds can grow a continually expanding base of customers. The same can be said for planting seeds for an expanding base of labor in your community. You don't have to climb to the mountaintop and scream that you're looking for great people to get applicants. All you have to do is:

1. Be a great place to work. (If this isn't the case, go back and re-read Chapter 2, as nothing else in this book will matter.)

2. Let a few key people in your community know exactly what you're looking for, because there's tremendous power in the network you already have.

You might be thinking, "But dude, I don't really know a lot of 'key' people."

Please understand that I'm not referring to being on a first-name basis with your city's mayor, or playing golf with the proprietor of the most successful business, or even grabbing coffee with the owner of the biggest house in town.

The "key people" we're talking about here are those that can connect you to the potential employees that *they* know.

Think about the places you frequently visit around your home and office: the supermarket, the drugstore, the big box retailer, the bank, and your local coffee shop. Maybe you frequent the ballpark, a fast food taco joint, or your kid's school. How many connections (or reconnections) with potential customers and job candidates did you make while you were out and about? How many could you have made with a simple smile and a handshake? How many of those connections could lead to word-of-mouth referrals to additional layers of connections?

I'm going to suggest that you have anywhere from ten to hundreds of community outreach opportunities each and every week right in front of you. Literally hundreds. And among them, there are connectors who can be—and who want to be—a gushing pipeline of job candidates for your business.

Imagine if everyone you run into on even a quick, casual basis (1) knew why your company is so great, (2) knew you were hiring, and (3) knew what kind of employee would make the best possible fit for your open positions. Imagine you discussed your hiring needs with people in line at the hardware store, acquaintances you ran into at the movies, the parents and coaches you saw at your kids' games and the parents and teachers you chatted with at parent-teacher night, the parishioners you greeted each week at your church, mosque, or synagogue, etc. Now imagine that each of these people genuinely liked you and cared enough about your search for great people that they told two friends, who told two friends, and so on and so on…

Networking Is a Long-Term Play

Networking is an essential part of marketing a business. The formula is pretty straightforward (though effective implementation may take some practice): Position yourself where your prospects and customers are likely to be. Then, make a dynamite first impression and a personal connection to as many prospects as possible. Be prepared with insightful questions, a knock-it-out-of-the-park elevator pitch, and a solid follow-up strategy. Show that you're passionate about your products and services, and focus on the value you provide to customers and the community. That's where the magic happens.

You can capture the same magic when you're recruiting. When you truly understand and believe beyond a doubt that your employees *are* your business and that you offer a fantastic work environment, you'll naturally start talking to people in your community about your hiring needs. These kinds of conversations will eventually come as second nature.

Your community is a wide-open field just waiting for networking seeds to be planted and cultivated. Networking is about organic growth, and it can take lots of patience and require outside-the-box thinking. It also can be a heck of a lot of fun, as well as personally and professionally rewarding.

Growing your community network starts with knowing and fervently believing in the ways in which your company differs from others in your industry and in your community. I'm not just talking about the products and services you offer. I'm also talking about the difference you can make by improving the lives of the individuals who work for you and the individuals and families who live and work around you.

Your networking success won't come by accident, and it certainly won't happen overnight. While you'll experience short-term wins along the way, the truth is that you're in for more of a marathon than a sprint. It can take years to establish a reputation in your community as someone who offers exceptional support to others without expectation of anything in return. Just keep building a track record of outstanding service to your customers, to your employees, and, last but not least, to your community.

Where and When to Network

In order to be a community outreach superstar, an employer needs to understand WHEN and WHERE to network.

As I mentioned earlier, a basic tenet of successful networking is to go where your prospects are—both business prospects and recruiting prospects. If your community is a wide-open field, you have limitless options. Because you don't have unlimited time, it makes sense to take advantage of the opportunities that occur naturally in the course of a day as well as set targets where you'll likely make the most important connections.

Breadth—connect anytime and everywhere. When and where are the best places to grow your network? In terms of breadth, it's anytime and everywhere. Each and every occasion that you spend time in your community is a chance to make a connection. When you're in line at the post office, strike up a conversation with the person next to you. When you're at the ballpark, reinforce connections with others rooting for the home team. Parents' nights at school can open the door to relationships with lots of members of the community as well.

When you become a networking master, candidates (and customers) will be drawn to you. That's the ultimate reward.

Kris Lareau, owner of the Office Pride Commercial Cleaning franchise in Visalia, California, told me, "Our reputation has grown so positive in the community that my operations manager was driving a company vehicle through a drive-through, and the person working the drive-through recognized the company and asked to apply for a job right then and there."

Where will you go this week in your community? How many connections will you make? How many connections of your connections might you be able to reach? Think about it—and then get out there and hunt!

Depth—dig deep at meetings, concerts, and events. In addition to moving broadly through the community in the normal course of events, you can target particular places for networking. These places can include chamber of commerce meet-and-greet events, meetings held by civic organizations (Rotary, Kiwanis, Lions), and industry-centric meetings and conferences. Work the room, investing time to get to know new contacts instead of simply hanging out with people you already know. Ask like-minded employers about their hiring challenges and success stories, and pocket some recruiting tips along the way.

Once you've found something that works in your community, stick with it and build on it. Then once you've established a strong reputation in your community, work to maintain it. Word-of-mouth marketing is gold.

How can you make yourself known as a steady contributor to the health, well-being, and growth of your community? Pick a few events and volunteer activities where you'll devote your money, time, and energy, and commit to these activities regularly so that community members begin to count on you and look forward to your participation and leadership. Sponsor the 5K run, give your employees the day off to pick up litter in local parks. Provide Thanksgiving meals to families in need or teach a class at the local community college on a topic with which you have solid expertise. The more you give, the more you get. (Not that that should be your primary motivator…)

If You're Looking to Hire Skilled Professionals, Start in Your Own Backyard

Brian Greenley, the owner and operator of the Littleton, Colorado, MAACO Auto Painting and Collision Repair franchise, is a prime example of the power of community networking. He has solidified his business as the place everybody in town goes to for collision repair—even those who own exotic luxury cars. On top of that, every auto repair tech in town (and out of town for that matter) wants to work for this particular MAACO.

To prove this, Greenley's MAACO has been the top revenue generator in a system of more than 500 MAACO franchises for nearly 20 years. His customer reviews are off the charts, and he has had the majority of his workforce with him for 15 years or longer—and we're talking about highly skilled and trained autobody collision technicians who are in high demand and very short supply.

Brian knows that successful recruiting can happen any-time, anywhere. He offers this advice: "You want great employees? Recognize when they're standing right in front of you and make them an offer!" By paying atten-tion to the people he engages with every day, Brian has successfully hired a waiter from his favorite steakhouse, an account rep from a local rental car company, and even the owner of another successful auto repair business who wanted to work for Brian so much that he packed up his own shop and is now employed with Brian.

How did this particular autobody shop grow to the juggernaut it is?

The answer is simple: When it comes to growing a community network, Brian Greenley starts with his employees. He recognizes that each employee has their own network, and he makes a point of knowing each person's families, hobbies and interests, and sources of happiness and frustration. He knows what inspires them to do their best.

When I toured Brian's shop, I watched him personally connect with his people. He commented on the score of the soccer game of one of his painter's sons. He asked one of his detailers if he enjoyed the Bruno Mars concert he had been to the previous weekend. He told one of his estimators to take off early because it was his wife's 35th birthday and he needed to shower up and take her to a nice dinner, which Brian paid for.

Regardless of how backlogged his business might get, Brian closes shop every day at 5:30 P.M. so his techs can go home and have dinner with their families. If one of his people decides to stay late to finish a job, Brian stays late with them to find out if they need help or if something else is on their mind. He wants to know if this employee is getting the mentoring they need, if they have the best tools for the job, if they need a specific kind of training, etc.

Brian Greenley is never on autopilot; instead, he's actively involved and showing he cares for his people every step of the way.

When Brian's employees are out in the community, what do you think they say about their company? You can bet that they share stories about being heard, appreciated, and cared for at work. Brian's employees are walking and talking advertisements for why MAACO in Littleton, Colorado, is THE place that anyone in the collision repair or restoration industry would want to call home.

...and on that, there's not even a "close second."

How to Network

In order to be a community outreach superstar, an employer also needs to understand *HOW* to network. I've included some ideas below.

1. Provide value first. Doing good and doing good business go hand in hand. It's one thing to have a value proposition, but it's another thing altogether to live your values in service. Actively demonstrate the pride you have in your community and the respect you have for all those who live and work in it. It's not about a quid pro quo; instead, it's about offering your resources without expecting anything in return. (In time, of course, you will reap the rewards as your community comes to realize that your company walks the talk. When they understand who you are at your core, they will rally around you.)

A logical place to start is considering how you can donate or otherwise use your core business competencies to sponsor community organizations that matter to you. If you run a corporate cleaning company, perhaps you could provide the high school football team with free services. If you're a caterer, lend a hand at local homeless shelters. If you run a printing shop, offer to print flyers for the local arts or film festival. You can play a vital role in helping local organizations achieve their mission while also promoting your business—win-win!

Over time, your reputation will grow, and your generosity will come full circle. Rick Pollock of Total Show Technology in Las Vegas, Nevada, for example, has established a fantastic relationship with his local church community by providing free audio-visual services, including lighting and sound equipment, for church services and events. He feels good about supporting his congregation and gives freely, without seeking new business or recruiting leads in return. He has nonetheless received recommendations for several new hires from church members who respect him and his business and know Total Show Technology is a great place to work.

2. Make it about them. American author and speaker John Maxwell stated, "They don't care what you know until they know that you care." This is true in life and business. A surefire way to create a positive impression and make yourself memorable is to focus on other people instead of spending all your time trying to sell them on why you and your company are so great (even when you really are great). Ask questions and sincerely listen to the answers. Hear what's on others' minds. Offer a shoulder to lean on in times of trouble or a congratulatory handshake when celebration is in order. Brainstorm ideas with someone who's struggling with a decision.

One memorable way to affirm a connection and let someone know you care is to follow up after an encounter. E-mail is nice, but it's hard to beat a handwritten note or card. I'm not terrific at remembering names, so I make it a point to jot down information from a conversation shortly after I meet someone. I make notes about their full name, what they do and where they work, mutual business interests, how many kids they have, their birthday or other big events coming up, etc. Then I follow up with a written card and, if it makes sense, include something related to our conversation that could provide benefit to them. This insert might be a recent business article or summary of research that the recipient might find useful. My goal is to start building bridges and to reinforce those I've already established.

3. Know the influencers. A smart networking strategy is to connect with the influencers in your community. Imagine that you're in the tenth grade, and you're the new kid at school. Your reputation will depend in part on who you hang out with. You may want to get to know the president of the student council, the cool kid in a rock band, the most talented techie, the lead in the school play, the track and field star, or the yearbook editor. The rules of community engagement are reminiscent of the rules you played by in high school. Finding and standing with people who have a finger on the pulse of your community can open many doors for your business and provide you with timely, relevant information on how you can best fill a niche and serve. And it'll help you fill your hiring funnel.

4. Be an influencer. A rung up the networking ladder is to actually *be* an influencer. You'll probably have to select your area of expertise within micro-communities to get started. For example, you may want to be known as someone who wholeheartedly supports the troops. You can get to know the military recruiters in the area and then hire returning military personnel. You can also visit nearby military bases, sponsor veterans' events, volunteer at the local VFW post, and run Veteran's Day specials or discounts on your products or services.

Being an influencer means people will seek you out for information and for your backing—and just to be seen with the cool kid on the community campus. That's good for your recruiting efforts and good for your business.

A Few Thoughts about Those Logo Shirts

An effective marketing move involves placing your brand where many people can see it. Bonus: The best strategies don't necessarily require the biggest investment. A good example is T-shirts or golf shirts that display your company logo.

You and your employees are all out in the community every day. Whether you realize it or not, your brand army is on the march. Companies pay for athletes to sport their logos. They hand out free shirts and other logo swag at community events. Some even incentivize employees to wear their clothes outside of work. Why? Because it's an inexpensive promotional tool that works!

Your company logo can be a surefire conversation starter. I was recently in a grocery line, and the woman in front of me was wearing a golf shirt with the logo of a local company that seemed vaguely familiar. She also had a tape measure strapped to her belt. As we waited in line, I asked if she worked in construction. She said she did, and we had a conversation about what it takes for a company to be successful in such a competitive industry and how people can earn a very good living doing construction work. She was a stellar brand ambassador, and I'll remember the name of the company and our positive conversation the next time I'm asked for a construction referral, I need construction help at Camelot Car and Dog Wash, or I'm asked about local jobs in construction.

And a shirt is not only a conversation starter; it can also be a brand builder. National Chimney, a leading manufacturer of steel chimney liners and components with seven factories throughout the United States, employs over 300 people. Owner and president Darin Bibeau wants everyone in every community in which they operate to know that they are a values-based company. Their impressive five core company values, each one beginning with the first letter of the acronym H-O-N-O-R, are printed in large type on the back of all employee T-shirts and hoodies. And to make sure those lofty values are always in practice, those core values are also printed on a colorful 2" x 3" plastic card that all employees carry with them to pass out to friends, family members, neighbors, and prospects. Bibeau told me this keeps his employees focused on living out those values at home and on the job, and it also attracts interest from people who want to work for an organization that aspires to these high values.

---

5. Tell your story. If your organization is the best of the best, then your employees are surely the reason why. Recognize them in house early and often. But don't stop there. Why not celebrate them in the community as well? Sing (or rather shout) their praises, and tell their stories to anyone who will listen. Doing so showcases the fact that you've built a great place to work, lets your employees know that you appreciate them, and bolsters your employees' self-esteem and loyalty.

Here's another thing: Many reporters in your local media outlets are hungry for good human interest stories. Perhaps one of your employees was recently reunited with their family because Ancestry.com told them about siblings they never knew about. Maybe an employee's parents just turned 100 or an employee's daughter just got a full-ride scholarship to Stanford. Maybe an employee just celebrated their 20th year with your company, or your entire team devoted five workdays in the past year to volunteer work (with paid time off courtesy of your company). If you've built your company into a great place to work, then good media attention is ready and waiting for you. Share those untapped stories.

6. Have fun. My final piece of advice is to enjoy the networking ride. This part of the job is about getting to know people and learning what makes your community unique. Heartfelt, ongoing networking will lead to personal and professional growth that will feed back into your company in ways you can't imagine. Through active networking, I've met friends who have stuck with me for decades.

Community Networking in Action

Below are some examples of business leaders who have leveraged the power of their community network.

"We've found success working with an AA group (Alcoholics Anonymous) that focuses on placing people in stable jobs to help them get back on track," says Angel Lara, a multi-unit owner of El Pollo Loco restaurants in Southern California.

The HR director for the Signal 88 private security franchise in the Tampa/Orlando area volunteers to teach night security "D License" classes. This allows him to establish relationships with people who are interested in pursuing careers as security officers.

Scott Anderson, the owner of a Massage Heights location in Lenexa, Kansas, gets his employees involved and excited about recruiting in their community. He'll pay his massage therapists to get a massage at another company in town. If that individual receives great service, they are instructed to give that therapist a business card and let them know that if they should want to explore opportunities available at Massage Heights, they should simply give Scott a call. He "doubles down" on this tactic by having his therapists get massages from the students at the local massage school and invite those students who are exceptional to call Scott and begin their career with Massage Heights. *(What an awesome tactic this is for getting a leg up on the competition!)*

Mark Silver, owner of The Cleaning Authority franchise in Spokane, Washington, has roots deep in his community. "We partner with many different organizations in town. We meet with the directors of those agencies quarterly so they are aware of our current need for employees. We partner with the YWCA Women-to-Work program, the Family Promise organization that helps transition homeless families in our community, and the local WorkSource Career Center. These kinds of organizations are always willing and eager to work with their clients to help them find and keep full-time employment. They are often not what we imagine our target candidates to be, but most of the time those we hire from these partners far exceed our expectations."

David Adams, the owner of the Aire Serv franchise in Victoria, Texas, is always on the lookout for students at the local tech schools, even those who have no HVAC training. That way, he says, he doesn't have to break a lot of previously engrained bad work habits. He told me, "I keep my eyes peeled everywhere I go. If I meet a young guy who is mechanically inclined and has a positive attitude, I'll approach him about the possibility of coming to work for me. Now if I find that the guy comes from a farming or ranching family, that's the 'trifecta' because farm and ranch kids know how to work and are typically as *strong as an ox*. We have a nickname for those guys. We call 'em *CORN FED BOYS!*"

Tim Nordquist, the fixed operations management consultant for Baxter Automotive in Omaha, Nebraska, connects with the Spanish-speaking community to determine what they utilize to attract employees and enlists their help to write "Help Wanted" ads in newspapers and make signs to post in their area.

PR Olson, owner of Olson Pest Technicians in Sioux Falls, South Dakota, shared how his customers help find techs for their company. "Our customers are some of our best recruiters. I instruct my team to ask each client if they know anyone that would want to work for us before they leave the site. That tactic has been really successful for us."

Tips and Tactics

The best-known brands invest heavily in marketing. Even billion-dollar companies like Coca-Cola advertise in order to stay at the top of everyone's mind. If yours is a smaller business, you don't need to invest a lot of money, but you should still build your brand power and visibility. The more your brand is recognized and respected by your neighbors (and their friends and their friends' friends), the easier it will be for you to recruit in your community.

Of course, you'll need to build real relationships with members of your community if you want to achieve real results. Here are some tips and tactics that can get you started:

- Remember that even when you're not recruiting, you're recruiting—anytime and everywhere. Promote your business by making sure you stand out within your community. Blending in won't help you land new business or new employees.

- Understand your employees if you want to find more people like them. Knowing what your employees want and what your community needs will help you use your unique value proposition to their advantage—and to yours.

- Invest time and resources in getting to know the influential people in your area. Better yet, become an influencer in your community.

- Share your business's and your employees' stories to help build employment brand awareness.

- Take time to find and establish connections with the media outlets in your area, and provide them with human interest content about your business and your employees. Publications love "feel good" stories. Your employees and current/future fans will love them too.

- Recognize that networking is a journey, not a destination. Once you've established a successful community support program, continue to nurture it and build upon it.

Chapter 10

RECRUITING STUDENTS
From High Schools, Colleges, and Trade Schools

began my career as a high school business teacher and coach. I was vocationally credentialed (a vocational credential is now called CTE, or Career and Tech Ed credential), which meant that the senior students in my classes could earn one academic credit for being employed in a part-time job. Those jobs, however, needed to be relevant to the material we were covering in my class, and the employer had to be willing to coordinate the student's job experiences with me and agree to provide frequent evaluation of the student's performance.

This worked out extremely well for the employer, as they had a student who was motivated by more than just a paycheck and would not quit their job without suffering come serious consequences at school. It also worked out great for the student because their teacher (me) was checking up on them every few weeks to make sure they were getting to do more than just one thing (e.g., being stuck behind a cash register, sweeping and mopping, making pizzas, etc.). And it worked out amazingly well for both parties because the student was able to apply the skills and behaviors they were learning in my class to their real-world job, and the employer had an employee who was receiving continual relevant training in both hard and soft skills at no cost to them.

I often wondered—as I still do—why this type of program isn't mandated for every high school student in every school in America. No matter how high the academic achievement is for any student, isn't the ultimate goal to transition them into a career, one in which they'll know HOW to work? But I digress…

You can tell that I am a fierce advocate and believer in the power of hiring students, especially those who may have a desire or an interest in learning something in your workplace that will help them move closer toward their career goals—or at the very least, learn things that will enable them to become more valuable to a future employer.

Now if you don't have jobs that a student could handle (though they likely can handle a lot more than you think) or you don't believe that a student could learn something really crucial to their future from their experience working for you, then skip this chapter and move on to the next one.

But if you're still with me, I'll spell out the obvious:

Yes, high school and college students are usually somewhat "green," meaning they don't have a wealth of work experience. Many don't know how to work, because they've never been taught to work. That's a very general statement, and there are many exceptions to it that we're not going to debate right now. But whether or not you agree or disagree with it, this actually can be a very good thing for you because their lack of work history means they haven't formed a lot of bad work habits and therefore they can be more easily inculcated with a good work ethic—one that they learn from you. (Awww. This almost seems altruistic, doesn't it?)

And yes, with the ever-increasing minimum wage mandates, students in their teens and early 20s are no longer a source of "cheap" labor. They do, however, possess great energy, and most are street-wise and tech-savvy, able to learn quickly and adapt to frequent changes. And look how fast your business is changing.

If you've never thought of hiring high school and college students, it may be time for you to strongly consider this very large pool of eager young talent in your community. I say this both as a former educator and also from firsthand experience. When my wife, Lori, and I were hunting for the "perfect fit" for Camelot Car and Dog Wash, we found Brady at the Colorado School of Mines. And when he graduates and moves on, I'll head back there to find his replacement.

It may not come as a surprise that connecting with educational institutions is a good—even great—recruiting strategy. Particularly in today's tough labor market, employers who know how to navigate relationships with schools definitely have a leg up on the competition when it comes to building a pipeline of qualified candidates—one that, if managed correctly, can produce great results year after year after year.

What might come as a surprise, however, is the sheer number of organizational options available to improve your candidate pool. At the top of the list, of course, are high schools, community colleges, and four-year colleges and universities. The list also includes adult education and private institutions in the training and credentialing space, as well as targeted online sites for high school students and other candidates. As a former educator, I can say with certainty that many dedicated and talented professionals in these educational systems are collaborating with employers to change the game in the current economy.

Here, I'll introduce the range of options available for finding employees who are good matches for your company, both today and in the future. I'll also share strategies you can adapt to effectively build win-win situations with learning organizations, along with examples from some of the amazing employers I've met.

Two Things to Know Before You Begin

1. It helps to know what you're hunting for. Earlier, I emphasized that you can find what you're looking for only when you actually know what you're looking for. Don't fish. Hunt. And don't lump all students into one general category. Students are not all the same and you should not recruit them as if they are.

Start by documenting the competencies (knowledge, skills, capabilities, and attitudes) that will lead to successful performance in a particular job you are seeking to fill. Doing so will set your company, teams, and new hires up for success. Further, this upfront clarity will help you communicate with the schools and educators and also the job candidates about the kind of students you're seeking to hire. Identifying the keys to effective job performance will enable your organization to mature and lead to a better job-student match.

The great thing is that you don't need to write a complex job description from scratch. A good place to start is O*NET, short for the Occupational Information Network. Sponsored by the U.S. Department of Labor, this free resource is designed to be the primary source of occupational information in the country. Many educators and workforce development experts are familiar with and regularly use this service. It has a searchable database covering almost one thousand jobs. Information on each job includes details about tasks to be performed, required skills and capabilities, technologies used, work activities, work styles, and work values. Each job write-up also contains state and regional wage information, as well as recommended educational and credential requirements.[7]

Once you have a draft job description (possibly adapted from O*NET), ask people who know the job well—those already performing the job, direct managers, and others—to validate the specific requirements for the job at your organization. Once you've defined exactly what the job requires, you're ready to hunt for students who can be great fits for the jobs you have available.

2. You should give before you ask. Why didn't I just hang my "Help Wanted" sign in the hallways of the School of Engineering at Colorado School of Mines? Why didn't I just go up to professors and ask if they knew a student who wanted a job at my car wash? I certainly could have done one or both…

---

7   I'll talk more about O*NET in other chapters.

Instead, I chose to *give* before *asking*. "Hey, my name is Eric. Please come try out my new car wash! Here's a free wash coupon. By the way, do you have a dog?" I wanted to form a relationship, or at least get on someone's good side, before asking them for a favor. We all get asked for things all the time. And maybe you are a nice person who always tries to say *yes* but is too busy to say *yes* to every request and so some or many are forgotten. However, I bet you are more likely to return a favor to someone who has done something for you, right?

So don't just go to a school or institution hat in hand telling them you want to hire students. A lot of employers already do that, as witnessed by the endless "Help Wanted" signs students pass every day. Instead, go out of your way to form a relationship with the school, or the department, or more specifically, the instructor who could introduce you to the student(s) you most want to hire. Imagine how much easier it will be for you to make an "ask" if you are supporting their program or their classes by volunteering your time and/or resources in some manner. Could you, by chance, be a judge for some type of student competition they are involved with? Could you be a guest speaker for a class they are teaching? Could your business sponsor their school play, or sport, or activity? What is it you can do or offer them as a way to forge a mutually beneficial relationship?

Start by knowing what you're hunting for, and give before asking.

Here are some prime hunting grounds for you:

High Schools

When it comes to the level of education required for your open positions, you want to screen people in, not out. Begin by asking yourself if candidates *really* need a GED or associate degree for the job. After you've defined the requirements for a particular job, including the level of education needed to perform that job, it will be easier to identify which learning organizations to approach.

Depending on the job in question, you might start with high schools. The education system in the United States, as designed by the Founding Fathers, is decentralized. That means that state systems and the 13,600 school districts vary, as do the private schools, charter schools, magnet schools, online schools, and home school networks that serve about 56 million students in K–12 classrooms. Since collaboration with high schools has no one-size-fits-all formula, you'll have to do some homework. Below, I'll give you some instruction that you can adapt to your community.

Offer internships. An internship is when a student works for a company on a short-term basis. The company gains an employee, and the student gains experience and an opportunity to explore career options. The position can either be paid or unpaid, but paid internships are always more attractive to students. (Duh.) Companies that proactively implement summer and year-long internship programs often gain access to a talent pool for jobs both now and in the future.

To build an effective internship program, try partnering with high school career centers that can make students aware of internship opportunities and assist with logistics. In addition, align the internship position with responsibilities appropriate for high school-level skills (e.g., technology use and administrative tasks). Internships are also an opportunity for you to reinforce the people skills that employers are looking for (and often report they can't find in graduates), such as teamwork, communication, problem-solving, and critical thinking.

Not every high school student will continue on to higher education, so your intern could turn into a full- or part-time employee. When you provide students with a first-time, meaningful, engaging professional experience, they will remember you as an employer-of-choice down the road, even if they continue with their education instead of taking on a full-time job. And they may refer other qualified candidates to you or return someday with a newly minted diploma or certification that makes them even more valuable.

Connect with guidance counselors. Most high schools have career or college guidance counselors. These individuals may be able to connect you with students interested in internships or jobs, as well as online and other resources and events where you can promote opportunities. Keep in mind, however, that the average student-to-counselor ratio is 482:1, so accessing these valuable resources takes patience.

Here's one strategy: invest time in volunteering to participate on a business advisory council or serving as a student mentor. In doing so, you may find yourself closer to the front of the line. Here's another strategy: offer job shadowing opportunities at your company to high school counselors and other high school educators so they can observe firsthand the knowledge and skills required for your open positions and get a sense of your organizational culture.

Connect with career and technical education programs or centers. As a former CTE instructor, I could not encourage you with more fervor to pursue this avenue.

Today's career and technical education is not your father's (or your grandfather's) wood shop class. Millions of high school and college students are enrolled in CTE-related classes at thousands of high schools and community colleges in every state in the nation. These courses are split into 16 career clusters that apply to different high-demand careers:

1. Health science
2. Business
3. Sales
4. Finance
5. Information technology
6. Science, technology, engineering, and math
7. Manufacturing
8. Logistics
9. Hospitality
10. Government
11. Law

12. Agriculture
13. Human services
14. Construction
15. Training
16. Arts, audio/visual technology, and communications

If your business fits into one or more of these categories—and I've yet to encounter one that doesn't—being unaware of the multitude of ways CTE programs and students can bolster your workforce in this labor shortage is an ignorance you can ill afford.

Volunteer for career awareness programs. Most school systems have career programs, some starting as early as kindergarten. One way to help build your brand is to volunteer to participate in high school programs and career initiatives in earlier grades.

Educate parents. Parents play a huge role in directing the career path of their children. Look for opportunities such as parent-teacher association (PTA) meetings to educate parents about jobs and career opportunities in your business and industry.

Outside-the-Box High School Recruiting Strategies

Below are some additional strategies employers in my network have used to partner with high schools.

Field trips. Scott Myatt owns Myatt Landscaping Concepts in North Carolina. To inspire interest in landscaping as a career, Scott offers half-day field trips for high school students, including a tour of his main facility. During these events, he shares information about the landscaping business and leads a hands-on session to give students the opportunity to try out some of the equipment and experience other aspects of careers in landscaping.

Build a pipeline. Jason Ingermason, owner of a Freddy's Frozen Custard & Steakburger franchise in Kansas, partners with local schools and college administrators to create a pipeline of professionals looking to launch on-the-job training initiatives. He offers internship opportunities for students who want to pursue careers in departments such as marketing and accounting.

Key connectors. Don DeMario, owner of a Bonanza and Ponderosa restaurant franchise in Harrisburg, Illinois, makes a practice of introducing himself to the cooperative education teachers and guidance counselors at the high schools in his area. He tells these key connectors what it takes for students to thrive in his business and lets them know that he's more than willing to work around the sports, theater, clubs, band, and other school activities that complicate the schedules of students who may want part-time jobs. Says Don, "A great employee for two days a week is better than an average or poor one for seven!"

Faculty retreats. Shane Collins, general manager of Bill Collins Ford Lincoln in Louisville, Kentucky, hosts high school faculty retreats at the dealership to show educators how the retail auto industry has evolved over the years. He believes these teachers are able to draw upon the information they learn when they encounter students who might be well suited for a career in automotive retail.

"Build My Future" events. G5 Enterprises, a company based in Nixa, Missouri, installs insulation and exterior building products. The company's president, Maribeth Gardner, sends representatives to an annual event called Build My Future. Schools from across Southern Missouri participate in a day of hands-on activities representing architecture, construction, bricklaying, heavy equipment operating, virtual reality simulations, welding, and more. The most recent Build My Future event brought in close to 2,000 high school students from the surrounding areas to experience a variety of skilled trades and learn about job opportunities. After each event, G5 leaders compare notes about students they've met to determine how to proactively recruit the best prospects.

Trade Schools and Community Colleges

Community colleges—also called junior colleges and technical colleges—are two-year institutions of higher education. Approximately 1,400 colleges in all 50 states and the territories offer students accessibility and flexibility when it comes to schedules, course loads, and costs.

Community colleges can be valuable partners for employers looking for workers, including smaller businesses. They're well-positioned to help address the current labor shortage by developing skilled and certified candidates. Better yet, most receive funds from states to invest in the training and development of candidates and to transition them into the workforce.

Community College Recruiting Strategies

Below are some strategies employers in my network have used to partner with community colleges.

Connect with local community college staff. Meet with staff to learn about the services they offer and to see if collaboration might work for your organization.

Recruit candidates. Many colleges are positioned to assist with recruiting candidates, often at low or no cost. This assistance can include organizing job fairs, offering assessments for technical and employability skills, and participating in interview training.

Learn about training and development programs. Most colleges have funds to cover training and development programs, including programs customized for your industry and even your company.

Post jobs and internships on community college websites. Most community colleges have an Employer Relations (or similarly titled) section on their website where you can post job openings. The sites usually include recruitment guidelines (e.g., the employer must be a legitimate place of business, be an equal opportunity employer, and comply with affirmative action principles).

Hire apprentices. An apprenticeship involves student on-the-job training and usually some related classroom learning. A student who completes an apprenticeship generally receives a professional certification. Registered apprenticeships in the United States cover more than one thousand occupational areas, including construction, health care, law enforcement, and manufacturing.

Community colleges are becoming more actively involved with apprenticeships. The American Association of Community Colleges, for example, has partnered with the U.S. Department of Labor on an initiative to increase the number of apprenticeship opportunities. The initiative identifies, validates, and promotes successful workforce development models that can evolve into full apprenticeship programs.

Customize a recruitment program. Most community colleges will work with employers to customize their own recruitment and development program. States support workforce development through various grant programs run by partners, including community colleges. These grants include funds for schools to provide customized services to employers. Available funds vary from state to state.

Leading the Charge in North Carolina

One example of an innovative program is the North Carolina Manufacturing Institute (NCMI), an initiative to help regions and employers in North Carolina develop and retain workers in order to build a talent supply chain for manufacturing jobs. The program builds a pathway for people to acquire skills and access good jobs in their local communities, linking and leveraging the assets of multiple North Carolina counties to solve a growing gap between regional job seekers and available positions. Manufacturing companies work with educators to ensure they teach needed skills. Companies are asked to endorse the certified production technician program, promote the program, and hire program graduates.

Students, in turn, attend the institute for free (no experience required) and can become certified production technicians in eight weeks. Craig Lamb, vice president of corporate and continuing education at Rowan-Cabarrus Community College in Salisbury, North Carolina, reports that almost 90 percent of NCMI graduates find full-time jobs within one month of graduating.

For starters, students are guaranteed job interviews. When I visited the college, staff were organizing for a "reverse job fair." Instead of company representatives sitting at tables with candidates circulating, each graduate of the institute has his or her own table. Employers sign up in advance to circulate and interview the candidates. "It's not unusual for a graduate to come out of a job fair with multiple offers," one organizer told me. When a manufacturer hires a graduate, they pay a fee into a fund that supports scholarships for future students.

Four-Year Colleges and Universities

Four-year colleges and universities may not be the first places you think of when hunting to fill perceived unsexy and hard-to-fill jobs. But don't overlook them as a resource. It was at the venerable Colorado School of Mines where Lori and I found Brady, who wanted to work his way through school. (More than 70 percent of college students work while attending school.) In addition to career centers and internships, you can explore ways to position your offerings to appeal to college students.

Spotlight on Sports

Brian Stern, owner of a Two Men and a Truck franchise in the Boston area, sends letters to local college and high school wrestling, basketball, football, and other coaches to describe the benefits students can gain by working for his business. He has convinced many area coaches that their athletes will become more disciplined and focused and start the athletic season in better shape when they work at Two Men and a Truck during their off-season.

By contacting local athletic departments at Division III colleges and forging relationships with minor league and arena football teams around the country, Roger Panitch, owner of a College H.U.N.K.S. Hauling Junk & Moving® franchise based in Atlanta, has created a pipeline for "perfect fit" employees—big guys who enjoy moving heavy things. Roger notes that the guys he interviews and frequently hires look like NFL lineman, and they have the team-first mentality that it takes to succeed in the moving and storage business.

Adult Education and Literacy Programs

In the United States, about 35 million adults have low literacy levels, including 20 percent of those who have a high school diploma.

Typical adult learners are in their 30s, have a family, and may be holding down two or more jobs to make ends meet. Many adult learners have the motivation, attitude, work ethic, and ability to perform successfully in entry- and mid-level jobs with career potential. They tend to offer a wealth of life experience and have proven perseverance by working while going to school.

Generally speaking, adult education programs are an undervalued recruiting resource. These publicly and privately funded programs help adults improve their English language, verbal, and math skills. Students often work toward a credential (e.g., GED or high school equivalency) in order to transition to employment or post-secondary education.

Publicly funded programs in adult education are typically connected to the more than 2,500 One-Stop Career Centers (also called American Job Centers) around the country, providing resources in their communities for skills development, credentialing, and career readiness. Furthermore, non-profit literacy programs, including community-based programs, work with a variety of adults who may need more individualized attention. Between community-based programs and publicly funded programs, you should be able to find ample opportunities to partner with an initiative to attract prospective workers.

Adult Education and Literacy Program Recruiting Strategies

Below are some strategies employers in my network have used to partner with adult education and literacy programs.

Identify employer-friendly providers. Get the names of local adult education and literacy providers that have a track record of working with employers in order to identify potential employees or upskill incumbents with ambitious career goals. These providers want to hear from employers!

Educate providers about your business. Invite representatives of local basic education programs to visit your company to get a sense of what you're looking for in employees and what short- and long-term opportunities are available.

Be Clear, Be Visible, and Be a Real Partner

Be clear and specific about what your open positions require, especially regarding levels of proficiency and certification. Be visible in your community as a supporter of education and training for career advancement and personal development. And make successful partnerships with educational institutions a top priority.

Effectively attracting students to your organization may require some innovative thinking, but I think you'll find that the payoff can be big in terms of business outcomes. My guess is that if you look, you'll find educational employment initiatives in your area, along with educators open to brainstorming ways to partner with you to build your employee pipeline and help you recruit and retain valued workers.

Chapter 11

NAVIGATING WORKFORCE INVESTMENT SYSTEMS

You're driving down the highway on a sunny Monday morning with one thing on your mind: you need to find your next hunting ground for employees—and fast. Suddenly, a billboard catches your eye.

Hey Employer!
Are You Looking for Qualified Workers?

Someone's been reading my mind, you think. A mile down the road you see another sign:

Applicant Screening, Referrals,
Training, and Additional Resources.

You need all of the above. Intriguing. But of course, there's got to be a catch. The next billboard reads,

Dedicated Workforce Professionals
Are Waiting to Help You!

Aha! There's the catch! You figure that in order to get this hiring show on the road, it's going to cost you an arm and a leg to staff these "Dedicated Workforce Professionals" (a.k.a., expensive consultants). You should have known. After all, there's no such thing as a free lunch.

You keep driving, and then you pass a flashing billboard that almost makes you slam on your brakes:

All This at No Additional Cost to You!

No *additional* cost? You mean, you've already paid for this somehow? Now your mind is bursting with questions. What's the deal here, anyway?

Before your exit, you see one final billboard in this series that reads:

Your Tax Dollars Are at Work
at Almost 2,400 American Job Centers across the U.S. Visit Us Today at Careeronestop.org!

As it turns out, these dedicated workforce professionals are waiting to help you because your tax dollars (and the tax dollars of everyone else you know) already paid for them. Yet, until today, you probably didn't know you had made such a sound investment. And very likely, you haven't taken advantage of the opportunities afforded to you as an employer.

So, unless you've already tapped into this deep source of trained labor in your community, allow me to share some little-known secrets about how you can put your tax dollars to work *and* make it much easier to hunt for the great employees you need to hire.

Federal Workforce Initiatives in a Nutshell

The US government invests heavily in workforce development (to the tune of billions of public dollars). To that end, over the decades the US Congress has passed the following legislation to help workers find jobs and help employers find workers:

- The **Wagner-Peyser Act**, signed into law by President Franklin D. Roosevelt in 1933, established a system of employment services across the country designed to get people back on their feet and into jobs during the Great Depression.

- The **Manpower Development and Training Act of 1962** was signed by President John F. Kennedy, who said that "large scale unemployment during a recession is bad enough, but large scale unemployment during a period of prosperity would be intolerable." The act included plans to retain and retrain workers displaced by technological advancements.

- The **Comprehensive Employment and Training Act**, signed into law by President Richard Nixon in 1973, gave people jobs in the public service that would help them build skills they could transfer to work in the private sector or other subsidized jobs.

- In 1982, President Ronald Reagan signed the **Job Training and Partnership Act**, which authorized programs to provide training to individuals with serious barriers to employment.

- President Bill Clinton signed the **Workforce Investment Act** in 1998, which built on previous legislation to establish state and local workforce investment systems. The goal was to improve workforce quality and encourage the hiring and retention of workers.

The most recent major piece of workforce legislation is the **Workforce Innovation and Opportunities Act** that was passed by Congress and signed into law in 2014 by President Barack Obama. In his remarks at the signing ceremony, the president said that the mission of the legislation was to "Train Americans with the skills employers actually need, then match them to good jobs that need to be filled right now.... What we want to do is make sure where you train your workers first is based on what employers are telling you they're hiring for. Help business design the training programs so that we're creating a pipeline into jobs that are actually out there.... [T]he bill I'm signing today and the actions I'm taking today will connect more ready-to-work Americans with ready-to-be-filled jobs."

The Workforce Innovation and Opportunities Act requires states to align workforce development programs so that job seekers acquire skills and credentials that meet employers' needs. It also increases the quality and accessibility of services that job seekers and employers receive at their local American Job Centers, helps match employers with skilled workers, and promotes work-based training. Essentially, it's designed to improve our nation's public workforce system; help all Americans, including youth and those with significant barriers to employment, attain high-quality jobs and careers; and help employers hire and retain skilled workers. The act goes a long way toward supporting even the most ambitious employer recruiting and hiring initiatives.

Oddly, however, only a small fraction of employers take advantage of the public services that are readily available. I'm guessing that there are a number of reasons why this is true.

Businesses all over the country are scrambling to find workers and are looking for help. Some employers are reluctant to engage with government programs, thinking they'll get tied up in red tape and bureaucracy. I've spoken with business leaders who are concerned that they may end up on Big Brother's radar, which could lead to an investigation into their hiring and businesses practices by the U.S. Department of Labor or other government entities. Some think it will take too much time and effort to get involved with workforce organizations—that it won't bring a sufficient return on investment. Still others have heard that finding qualified workers through a government program is like looking for a designer dress in a thrift store—while it could happen, it's unlikely.

Finally, some employers simply don't know about the opportunities available or how to start accessing the many services offered courtesy of our tax dollars. While your peers may not be in the know regarding the free services provided by workforce partners, you're now aware that valuable, free resources are at your disposal. And that gives you a leg up on much of the competition.

Do Your Employees Qualify for the Earned Income Tax Credit?

Are you familiar with the Earned Income Tax Credit (EITC)? It's a significant, refundable tax credit geared toward helping working individuals and couples in the low-to-moderate income range. Workers need to file tax returns to receive the credit, and according to the National Council of State Legislatures about 20 percent of those eligible don't claim this benefit. That adds up to millions of people who are missing out!

The amount of tax credit benefit depends on a recipient's income and number of children. For example, the maximum amount of credit for tax year 2019 was as follows:

- $6,557 with three or more qualifying children
- $5,828 with two qualifying children
- $3,526 with one qualifying child
- $529 with no qualifying children

These amounts are indexed annually for inflation, and eligible taxpayers can file retroactively for up to the past three years.

Here are a couple of examples of how the EITC works based on 2019 data from the Internal Revenue Service.

- A married couple filing jointly with three children has an income of $55,592 (earned and adjusted gross income) or less. The maximum credit they have earned: $6,557.

- A single head of household or widow earns $15,570 or less and has no children. The maximum credit he or she has earned: $529.

When you're talking with current employees or onboarding new workers whose salaries fall within the low-to-moderate range, make sure they're aware of the EITC. You may even be able to partner with local nonprofits that promote EITC awareness campaigns or services that provide tax assistance.

For instance, each year in late January the IRS promotes EITC Awareness Day to encourage those eligible to apply for this benefit. Partners in this effort include businesses, community organizations, elected officials, state and local governments, schools, and other stakeholders. A Partner's Outreach Toolkit and other materials are available at the IRS website. Not-for-profit organizations in many communities also provide free tax preparation services for those who may be eligible for the EITC. (As just one example, the Cuyahoga EITC Coalition in Ohio supports 25 sites across the county that offer high-quality, free tax preparation services.)

Test-Driving Today's Workforce Investment Systems

I wanted to find out for myself what potential exists under the Workforce Investment and Opportunities Act, so I visited multiple state websites (for example, Washington, North Carolina, and Texas). The wording and specifics of each site vary, but here are some of the standard services that I found offered to businesses:

- Job applicant screening and qualified candidate referrals
- Information on tax credits and incentives for employing workers from particular groups
- Information about federal bonding (insurance for hiring at-risk workers)
- Space to conduct job interviews
- Help arranging job fairs
- Access to hiring and other events
- Employee training resources
- Workshops on employer-related subjects
- Layoff/closure prevention services for employers
- Up-to-date labor market facts and projections

Most of these services are offered at no cost to employers.

Let me say that again to clarify. These vast resources aren't going to cost your business a nickel outside of the tax dollars you've already paid.

If you're remotely interested in pursuing these kinds of opportunities, visit Careeronestop.org, a website sponsored by the U.S. Department of Labor that includes a search engine to find any of almost 2,400 local American Job Centers nationwide. The site requires no sign-up or log-in, and information is easy to search for and locate.

To demonstrate how simple this government-sponsored process is (and let it be known, this is the first and only time you'll ever see "simple" and "government" in the same sentence), I selected at random a CareerOneStop center in Washington state (they're called WorkSource centers there) to test whether or not the center could truly support an employer's recruiting efforts.

As I dialed the center, I expected to hear a recorded message. Instead, a very friendly staff member picked up the phone. I explained that I was a small businessperson interested in their recruiting and hiring services. Within seconds, the staff member connected me with Jade, a specialist in recruiting. Jade asked a few questions about my needs, and then in clear, easy-to-understand language (not government or corporate jargon) she explained what the center offered in terms of job posting and referral services.

Jade added that they were hosting a veteran's job fair that very day and that I would be welcome to attend the fair, along with a variety of hiring events frequently held in the area. She also told me about a featured employer program to promote employers to the local community and offered to send me details and provide any follow-up information I might need.

By the end of our conversation, Jade had already e-mailed me information about the following services available to employers at no cost:

- **Job postings on the WorkSource Washington website, WorkSourceWA.com.** Employers that post jobs with WorkSource gain access to Washington's largest pool of active job seekers, along with the candidate pool from Monster.com. Employers can post jobs for free, work with local recruiters to hunt for the right candidates, and search for specialized and general talent—all from one website. To start, employers can create a profile and watch videos on how to post jobs and manage candidates.

- **Spotlight on your jobs.** Spotlights include information on hiring events, employer forums, and how to become a featured employer.

- **YesVets Program.** This program recognizes employers who make extra efforts to hire veterans and holds an annual ceremony on Flag Day (June 14) to acknowledge these business partners.

- **Employer incentives, guidance, and programs.** This included links to information on the following:

  » Work Opportunity Tax Credit fact sheet

  » Fair Chance Act

  » Labor and Industries Preferred Worker Program

  » Apprenticeships for employers

  » Customized training programs

  » Paid Family and Medical Leave

  » SharedWork Program

All in all, talking with the WorkSource Washington representatives and receiving such detailed information made my call that morning one of the best customer service experiences I've had in a long time. With their help, I was armed with both substantial resources and clear next steps. Color me impressed.

Workforce Investment Partners

When you tap into government services, you also enter into a network of additional workforce partners. Basically, state workforce plans and local workforce areas are also connected to the Workforce Innovation and Opportunities Act. Every community across the country is affiliated with a local workforce investment board whose mandate is to implement the legislation. The board oversees the network of almost 2,400 American Job Centers and guides the federal, state, and local funding to programs that meet the needs of employers and serve current and potential employees.

By law, employers must comprise at least half of the membership of each workforce investment board. Other members can include representatives from educational institutions, labor unions, and organizations with workforce as part of their mission, such as Goodwill Industries, United Way, and other community-based entities.

Tips and Tactics

At the end of the day, as you drive home thinking about what you have learned from the billboards on the side of the road, keep in mind that while hunting and hiring are tough, you don't have to go it alone. Workforce investment systems can take care of a lot of the heavy lifting for you, freeing you up to focus on becoming a recognized employer of choice in your community, nailing down the qualifications for each open position, and interviewing candidates to find the right fits for the jobs.

Here are a few tried and tested tips for how you can use workforce investment systems to help you achieve your recruiting and hiring goals:

- Contact your local American Job Center or CareerOneStop center through Careercenter.org and identify the services that best meet your needs.

- Make an appointment to meet or talk with a business or outreach representative at the center, and do your research ahead of time to review resources and prepare questions in order to give you the best chance to find qualified employees.

- Determine which workforce partners best match your hiring needs. The mix of organizations in local workforce networks varies from community to community, so ask the center representative about the partners in your area that may be best positioned to meet your needs. In one region, it might be the local Goodwill training program. In another, the United Way may be known as a key workforce leader. A local faith-based welfare reform initiative could be a valuable resource in another part of the country.

- Get involved on the inside track. Earn the reputation as an *employer of choice*, and then promote that in your community. Since workforce investment systems are designed to be driven by employers, consider getting your organization's name out there by acting as a resource to education and training programs or serving on a workforce investment board. This takes some time, but the result will prove well worth it!

Chapter 12

AN ARMY OF TALENT
Why, Where, and How to Hire Veterans

Trevor was born in 1982 and grew up in rural South Carolina. He was a decent high school athlete and an average to above-average student with an endless curiosity about how things work. Starting in middle school, Trevor spent all his spare time outside in the garage with his dad, tinkering with cars and motorcycles. At age 16, he decided he wasn't cut out for school, so he took a job in a local auto repair shop. He went on to earn a GED and lived what he called a "satisfactory" life.

Then 9/11 happened. Out of a sense of patriotism and duty, Trevor joined the U.S. Army. It was there where he finally found himself and took his mechanical skill set to a whole new level.

During boot camp, Trevor thrived on the constant physical and mental challenges thrown at him, as well as the bonds he developed with his fellow recruits. He served multiple tours in Iraq and Afghanistan. His Military Occupational Specialty—or MOS, as it's commonly known—was Wheeled Vehicle Mechanic. He was responsible for supervising and performing maintenance and recovery operations on wheeled and armored vehicles. He had such a knack for getting badly damaged vehicles back in service that his Army pals gave him the nickname "Superwrench."

Although he had traveled to the other side of the planet, Trevor felt like he was home with his brothers.

After eight years of service, Trevor—like 55 percent of all soldiers—decided to transition back to civilian life. He visited CareerOneStop.org, the career, training, and job search website for the U.S. Department of Labor. The website provides job seekers, businesses, students, and career advisors with free online tools, information, and resources. Trevor also visited the American Job Center near his hometown and applied for a job as a maintenance mechanic at a manufacturing plant outside of Columbia, South Carolina.

Ramona, the hiring manager at the plant, was desperate for a highly skilled mechanic who wasn't intimidated by big industrial machinery. She needed a tech who had practical experience and could perform well under stress, adapt to frequent change, and work well with a very diverse group of employees.

Trevor's interview with Ramona went down like this:

RAMONA (HIRING MANAGER): Tell me about a time when you had to perform under high stress at work.

TREVOR: My work in Afghanistan required me to service our unit's vehicles. My specialty was working on the Humvees that our soldiers used to convoy to the local landing strip and run patrols, but there were also tanks and choppers needing repair and I needed to figure those systems out on my own. Our outfit lived and worked in an isolated area that often came under attack. The most stressful part was having to fix a Humvee that was damaged or needed preventative maintenance so it could leave for a mission the next day. There was no room for error. I had to make sure it would perform and get out the door on time and return the troops to safety without a hiccup.

Whoever came up with the phrase "good enough for government work" didn't know our outfit. Every day we worked to achieve our team's mission. I couldn't allow a vehicle to break down in the middle of Afghanistan. I didn't want to be the one responsible for any soldier being exposed to more danger than they already were in. I had to get my work done right the first time. Not letting my guys down was job number one.

RAMONA: Tell me about a time when you had to change plans to handle an unexpected event.

TREVOR: We changed plans just about every day, sometimes every hour. We regularly found ways to repair vehicles when we didn't have the parts on hand. We had to make parts fit with minor adjustments or "cannibalize" parts from vehicles that weren't running or weren't needed in the field immediately. Then we would replace the parts when new shipments came in.

With newer equipment, the user manual was sometimes missing or written by someone who had never worked in the field. We would put our heads together and translate what was needed to prep the vehicles for dust and heat unlike anything the folks in the factory that built the trucks ever experienced.

RAMONA: How did you complete projects and missions with soldiers, both superiors and subordinates, that you didn't like, or maybe even couldn't stand?

TREVOR: A lot of what I learned in mechanic school helped me understand how to fix our vehicles, but when I got out in the field—especially in Iraq—it was a whole new ballgame. I had to get up to speed quickly, make adjustments, and come up with workarounds. Some of the soldiers I was over there with were incredible, and others were total whackos. I couldn't hand-select who I worked with. It was a grab bag of all sizes, shapes, and colors, but we were all on the same team and had to mesh no matter what.

One day we got a new commander. We came up with various ways to describe the commander's leadership style, and "micromanager" fell short. It was more like "microscopic management," as we felt our every move was being monitored and criticized. It really sucked.

However, we put all of that aside and worked together to meet mission requirements and keep the commander happy. As the new guy on the block, I was elected to run interference, which I did for about six months. Eventually, "Mic" (short for "micro") got promoted, and we all celebrated, as we were able to go back to working as a "get 'er done," high-performance team.

Quite the interview, huh? You probably won't be surprised to hear that Trevor landed the job. His technical skills, along with his Army leadership skills, quickly established him as a top performer in the entry-level position. Today, he's part of the executive team at the 200-plus person plant, where he works as a maintenance department manager and leads a team of six skilled mechanics.

Today, Trevor also mentors students studying mechanics at the local community college. In addition, as a part-time entrepreneur, he restores classic cars in his garage on weekends. Trevor's 15-year-old daughter is right at his side, loving the work and totally absorbing her father's attention to detail.

Want a Sure Bet? Hire a Vet!

Some veteran-owned companies and other employers have an established record of—and reputation for—hiring vets. Other companies don't yet have the veteran recruiting thing down, and if they have a veteran or two on their payroll, it's purely by accident.

So wrap your brain around this: Almost 250,000 military members transition out of the Armed Services each year. And one of them could be your next superstar employee who's just waiting for you to reach out to them, bring them on board, and show them why your organization is the perfect home for them.

To be clear, I'm not suggesting that you hire veterans simply to thank them for their service. When it comes to hiring, you want to choose the right employees, and of all people, veterans understand the importance of making sure that they're a good fit for the job.

Here are some personal qualities and capabilities most veterans have developed or refined while serving their country:

Transferable skills. Veterans have received some of the best training in the world. Along with technical skills, veterans develop skills in leadership, teamwork, resilience, problem-solving, task execution, continuous improvement, and calculated risk-taking. Most veterans have also developed their ability to pick up new skills and competencies very quickly.

Leading and following. From the outset, military personnel learn to follow orders. At the same time, they're being prepared to assume leadership responsibilities. Any soldier could be in a situation where they have to step up, make quick decisions, and show leadership capabilities in challenging situations.

Teamwork. From the first day of boot camp, servicemen and women are expected to be dedicated team members and players, laying all prejudices and preconceived ideas aside. It's ingrained in them to think and act in terms of what can be done as members of—and for—the teams they serve, regardless of who is on those teams. This means interacting with people of all races, cultures, beliefs, ages, and ethnic backgrounds. Relying on their team members is a matter of survival. This commitment to teamwork and the ability to accept others for who they are, rather than what they are, could well be a key factor in the success of your business.

Safety orientation. Safety is the top priority in the military. Soldiers have an ongoing focus on safety and a heightened awareness of anything askew in their surroundings. They're also trained on how to assess situations quickly and respond effectively, including in emergencies. And when a disaster strikes or a crisis occurs, they can deal with the fallout and help you regroup.

Attention to procedures and detail. The military stresses respect for procedures, regulations, and details, both big and small. If you want your employees to adhere to a singular way of approaching tasks, put soldiers on the job.

Persisting under stress and pressure. Military personnel need to perform under difficult conditions and strict deadlines while constantly adjusting to change. These men and women are resilient under adversity. Persisting until they reach their objective is a foundational element of military training, one that serves them well in the civilian workforce. Veterans are likely to stay calm under stress and take the lead in focusing the team on top priorities.

Resourcefulness. Businesses are challenged to accomplish more with less in order to minimize waste and maximize profits. Veterans have often had to improvise and manage many variables in order to develop workable solutions to problems.

Work ethic and loyalty. The military develops a strong work ethic among its members. Most service members have a fierce loyalty to their branch of service. Consider the military values for each branch outlined below.

U.S. Army	Loyalty, Duty, Respect, Selfless Service, Honor, Integrity, and Personal Courage (LDRSHIP)
U.S. Navy and U.S. Marine Corps	Honor, Courage, and Commitment
U.S. Air Force	Integrity First, Service Before Self, and Excellence in All We Do
U.S. Coast Guard	Honor, Respect, and Devotion to Duty

Transitioning from Military to Civilian Life

Do any of the qualities and capabilities described above align with the competencies that you have identified for jobs at your company? I'm going to bet the answer is a resounding YES.

Before you hire a veteran, you may want to first identify what skills your job requires and then see which military occupational specialties (MOS) best match these requirements. The U.S. Department of Labor's Occupational Information Network (O*NET) is a tool that employers and service members in transition can use to align civilian jobs with military jobs.

Veterans can use O*NET to search for civilian jobs that match their MOS. For example, for persons in combat infantry roles, the top ten civilian jobs listed after an O*NET search are as follows:

- Aircraft Cargo Handling Supervisors

- Construction Laborers

- Correctional Officers and Jailers

- Emergency Management Directors

- Fire Inspectors and Investigators

- First-Line Supervisors of Construction Trades and Extraction Workers

- First-Line Supervisors of Correctional Officers

- First-Line Supervisors of Mechanics, Installers, and Repairers

- First-Line Supervisors of Office and Administrative Support Workers

- First-Line Supervisors of Transportation and Material-Moving Machine and Vehicle Operators

As a prospective employer, you can search the O*NET skills database to determine which military specialties correlate most closely with open positions. You can then recruit military veterans who are a good match for your needs.

Hiring Vets Can Provide Tax Incentives to Improve Your Bottom Line

When you hire a military veteran, you're likely getting an employee with the work ethic and competencies that can lead to the performance levels you're looking for. Hiring a veteran can also be a good business decision if your company can benefit from a tax break or a tax credit through the Internal Revenue Service's Work Opportunity Tax Credit (WOTC) program.

The WOTC was created in the mid-1990s to incentivize businesses to recruit and hire from the ranks of those who tended to have difficulty finding employment, such as welfare recipients and ex-offenders. Even with all of their documented qualifications, veterans were still impacted by the Great Recession. The veteran unemployment rate was 8.7 percent in 2010, and military veterans were added to the WOTC program in 2011. (As the economy improved and awareness has grown about the benefits of hiring veterans, the unemployment rate for veterans is now lower than that for non-veterans.)

Essentially, employers who hire unemployed veterans may be eligible for a tax incentive. The *Employer Guide to Hire Veterans* is a good resource. You can find more information at the U.S. Department of Labor's Veterans' Employment and Training Service website.

Strategies for Recruiting Veterans

I recently talked with the HR manager of a company that manufactures products out of concrete, including blocks, bricks, pavers, and retaining walls. When asked whether she actively recruits veterans, she said she would like to focus on veteran hires, as the company has 30 percent annual turnover and is hungry for reliable, long-term workers. However, she said that the head of the family-owned company has an old school mentality and pretty much hires anyone who walks in the door.

This manufacturing company's failure to tap into the veteran talent pool is a common enough story. But it doesn't have to be your story. Below, I'll highlight some strategies that can help your company become an employer of choice for veterans.

Build a Reputation as a Military-Friendly Organization

Establish your brand as military-friendly in one of the following ways (and don't be afraid to be creative!):

Start your search close to home. Do you already have one or more veterans on your payroll? If you don't know, find out. Start by reviewing their performance records, and you'll likely discover that they're among your top employees. Next, meet with these veterans and learn their stories. If they have a spouse or partner, you might meet with them as well. These individuals often provide key guidance and support in the family's big life decisions.

Shine a spotlight. Highlight the veterans who work for you and thank them for their service in newsletters, on your website, or at meetings and other gatherings. No one will ever think less about your business because you staff vets; in fact, many people will go out of their way to do business with you if they discover you hire former servicemen and women.

Lay out the red carpet. Your company can host open days for veterans (and spouses and partners) to enable them to learn about your business. Include a tour, Q&A sessions with leaders, and interactions with your veteran employees.

Encourage job shadowing. It's one thing to read on O*NET or another resource about how an MOS translates in the civilian world, but it's another thing altogether to give veterans the chance to experience civilian jobs firsthand. Through job shadowing, a veteran can follow an experienced worker for a day, a week, or longer, observing in detail how the job is performed.

Network and seek employee referrals. Employee referrals can also be an effective hiring strategy. Do your veteran employees have friends they can refer to you? Also ask within your community if anyone can introduce you to veterans looking for employment. At a recent chamber of commerce meeting, for instance, I learned of several employers who had hired veterans through introductions from chamber members.

Share your O*NET knowledge. Once you've used O*NET or other resources to search for veteran job candidates, you can share this information with workforce development organizations in your area (I discussed this topic in an earlier chapter). These intermediaries include your local American Job Center, your local Army Reserve or National Guard units, Goodwill Career Connection Centers, and temporary employment agencies.

As a proactive partner with some of these workforce development organizations, you can make it clear that you see veterans with the right skills and experience as valuable contributors to the success of your business.

Tap into existing job fairs and other events. You may be surprised at how many organizations help military personnel, veterans, and their spouses gain employment. (Conduct a Google search: try "veterans job fairs" or "small business hire veterans.") Below are just a few organizations to get you started.

- **Hiring Our Heroes Initiative.** The U.S. Chamber of Commerce launched the Hiring Our Heroes initiative in 2011. The vast majority of the Chamber's three million members nationwide are small businesses, and Hiring Our Heroes aims to help veterans, transitioning service members, and military spouses find meaningful employment opportunities with these businesses. Events across the country include hiring fairs, transition summits, sports expos, and career events for military spouses. Many of these events are held on military installations, where employers can connect directly with veterans. Sessions also include information on best practices that employers can adopt in recruiting, hiring, and retaining military veterans.

- **Veterans' Employment and Training Service (VETS).** The U.S. Department of Labor VETS mission is to prepare America's veterans and separating service members for meaningful careers by providing them with employment resources and helping protect their employment rights. The site includes links for employers such as the following:

  » **Veterans Hiring Toolkit.** This 28-page PDF contains information on employment strategies, best practices, tax incentives, and more.

  » **Find Qualified Vets.** Through this link (dol.gov/veterans/hireaveteran), employers can contact their local Veteran Employment Representative at 1-877-US2-JOBS and connect with their local CareerOneStop.

  » **RecruitMilitary.com.** RecruitMilitary is a subsidiary of Bradley-Morris, Inc., a major military recruiting company. Its stated mission is to "help employers connect with America's best talent—its veterans." RecruitMilitary hosts job fairs, job boards, a veterans' database, and more.

Veteran-Friendly Online Sites

Another way to find veterans looking to transition to civilian life is to post openings on veteran-friendly recruiting sites. In addition to the three resources mentioned above, here are a few more options:

- **Military.com** is one of the largest veteran and military online communities, with more than ten million members. The site includes a job board.

- **GI Jobs** (GIJobs.com) is geared toward military transition to employment or educational opportunities. Employers can use a subscription-based option to post jobs.

- **Hire Heroes USA** (HireHeroesUSA.org) is committed to veteran and military spouse employment. The organization manages a job board, hosts virtual job fairs, and offers other employment services.

After You've Hired a Veteran

Let's say you've hired a veteran and want to set your new employee up for success. Here are a few things to remember when working with military veterans.

Emphasize the purpose and mission of their work. Military personnel want to work for values-driven organizations, and they'll be more engaged if your company's mission and values align with theirs. How will their job positively impact customers, other employees, the company, the industry, the country? If your company shows continued commitment to your mission and values, as well as to civic values more broadly, veterans are more likely to give their all when it comes to job performance.

Develop veteran-specific onboarding. Effective onboarding for veterans can include sharing information about your organization that others may take for granted. Help them understand your company's organizational structure (remember, the military tends to be hierarchical), and invest the time to explain how your organization works. What's the chain of command? What formal and informal rules do they need to know? Proactively helping veterans understand what's expected of them—and what they can expect—can eliminate confusion and boost confidence.

Provide mentoring and support. Veterans are accustomed to receiving peer support, and in the service they often team up with a buddy who's committed to their success. Giving them an on-the-job mentor can help ensure a smooth transition. (Check within your organization to see if a veteran in your workforce could serve this role.)

Educate peers and leaders. Ensure that company leaders and team members understand that there may be some small hiccups initially as the veteran integrates into your culture. Encourage a give-and-take approach in terms of answering and asking questions to bridge any communication gaps. It's also not unusual for veterans to have more highly developed abilities than incumbents (including many leaders) in such areas as decision-making, resilience, and teamwork. The veteran's well-rounded skill set could well support your teams' development goals.

Share development opportunities. Veterans have worked in training organizations and are likely to be lifelong learners. Many will want opportunities to continually develop their skills and grow in their careers. If your business has defined career paths, work with veterans to clarify and map out steps toward their vision of the future.

Include military families. As I mentioned, military families are a key source of support to veterans and often continue to play critical support roles during the veteran's civilian transition. Veterans usually welcome and appreciate when you include their family members in company events and treat them as part of the corporate family.

Tips and Tactics

Are you ready to actively recruit veterans? You may find that they're your next superstars. Follow these tips and tactics to learn how to connect with veterans and integrate them into what are sure to become some of your organization's best-performing teams:

- Determine if veterans' skills, abilities, and experiences might be a good fit for your organization. (Hint: The answer will undoubtedly be "yes.")

- Use O*NET as a resource to match particular military occupations with your job needs.

- Explore ways to make your company more military-friendly—identify and highlight veterans already on your payroll, host open houses for veterans and their families, and promote job shadowing opportunities.

- Research veteran-specific job fairs, hiring events, and online hiring sites, as well as make veterans a key component of your employee referral and networking strategy.

- Find out if your company is a candidate for veteran hiring tax credits through the Work Opportunity Tax Credit program.

- Set new veteran employees up for success through customized onboarding, offering mentoring and support, providing development opportunities, and exploring ways to include military families in work events.

- Promote understanding among current employees about the differences between military and civilian cultures and the team benefits of bridging any gaps.

Chapter 13

BET ON BOOMERS:
Hiring Older Workers as Your Competitive Advantage

"Older, more mature employees are set in their ways and can't or won't learn new skills. They won't take direction from younger managers, and it leads to turnover. They move slower, and they won't keep up in today's fast-paced, high-tech work environment. They'll cost more in health care and benefits. And their *'Keep off my lawn, Sonny!'* grumpy attitudes will negatively impact my workplace culture."

Have you heard these kinds of comments floating around? Have you made some of them yourself?

If so, you're not the first employer to overlook older workers due to preconceived notions about this growing demographic and their value in the workplace.

If you've said similar things, or if you agree with what you just read about older workers, I'll cut you some slack. (And as a "boomer" myself, that doesn't come easily.)

The fact that you're reading this book means you're not overly set in your ways. You're the sort of leader who is open to new ideas when it comes to solving your labor woes. So let's start with busting some myths and mistruths about hiring applicants in their 50s, 60s, and even beyond.

Below are some common misconceptions that are debunked through the facts and realities about "older" employees.

Myth	Reality
Older workers are set in their ways and can't or won't learn new skills.	Experienced workers are interested in acquiring new knowledge and skills. And they are embracing technology. In 2000, only 14 percent of seniors 65 years of age and older used the Internet, and today the number is 67 percent. A report by the AARP (formerly known as the American Association of Retired Persons) shows that 80 percent of experienced workers would be interested in receiving technology training.

While some older workers may lack the tech-savvy skills that their younger colleagues possess, those older workers tend to have good leadership and face-to-face communication skills, as well as years of experience that most businesses can't afford to replace. |

Myth	Reality
Older workers won't stay on the job and will only increase problems with turnover.	Companies want long-term employees, so they may hire younger workers, thinking they're a better bet. But there's no guarantee those younger workers will stick around.
	According to the Bureau of Labor Statistics, workers between the ages of 55–64 stay on the job more than three times as long as those between the ages of 25–34. Workers over 50 are five times less likely to leave a job than those between the ages of 20–24. The reality is that older workers are more stable than younger workers. Older workers tend to stay in the workforce longer because they're more focused on job satisfaction than on moving up the ladder.
	According to another Bureau of Labor Statistics report, the length of time a worker remains with the same employer increases with the age at which the worker began the job.
Older workers will cost more in health care and benefits.	The degree to which this statement is valid probably depends on your company's health care plan. While health care is a big concern, these days older adults are in better health than ever before. In addition, the health benefits of individual workers can be offset by their having fewer dependents and their potential eligibility for Medicare. Older workers are also at lower risk of being injured at work and tend to take fewer sick days per year.

Myth	Reality
Older workers move more slowly and generally aren't up to the physical aspects of many jobs.	The Urban Institute reports that many older Americans, especially men, are choosing jobs that involve physical work. Common jobs for men over 62 include trucking and delivery, cleaning and janitorial work, and ranching and farming. For women over 62, common jobs that have physical components include personal care aide, child care worker, teacher, and home health aide.
Older workers are less likely to be engaged or have good attitudes.	An AARP report states that older workers are more engaged than younger ones. Hiring managers also rate this demographic highly in loyalty, dependability, and productivity. In essence, the right work for the right company gives older workers a sense of a purpose and the chance to draw upon skills and knowledge developed over a lifetime.

Powerful stuff, right? The thing is, a 70-year-old today isn't the same as a 70-year-old 30 years ago. And yet, problematic stereotypes persist, and some older workers are pushed out of their jobs or find it near impossible to find employment.

Age Discrimination and the Retirement Brain Drain

As I've mentioned, not long ago baby boomers ruled the world of work. In 2005, boomers (born between 1946 and 1964) held more than 50 percent of the jobs in America. Today, that number is less than 25 percent. More than 10,000 members of this generation are walking away from employment each day in what has been called the "silver tsunami," each taking with them decades of experience and wisdom.

However, many boomers are finding that the next chapter in their life's journey still includes some form of employment. In 2018, 2.9 million new jobs were documented by the U.S. Department of Labor—and nearly half of those jobs (1.4 million) were filled by individuals 55 years of age and older.

It's clear that many people are retiring later in life, and many retirees are returning to work. According to the AARP, it's also clear that older Americans are often overlooked when it comes to hiring. In a recent study, 61 percent of workers over age 45 say they have experienced or witnessed age discrimination on the job, and 91 percent say they believe such behavior is a common occurrence.

In another study, professors at Tulane University sent out 40,000 fake résumés in response to 13,000 real job listings for lower-skilled jobs such as administrative assistants, janitors, and sales associates. The résumés were identical with two distinctions—one included indicators of applicant gender (e.g., first name) and varying ages (e.g., graduation year and years of experience).

The study found that older individuals, particularly women, were less likely to hear back from prospective employers than younger individuals. Women aged 64–66, for example, were 47 percent less likely to receive a response to applications for administrative jobs than those aged 29–31. For sales positions, the difference was 36 percent.

Many employers are experiencing what has been called a "retirement brain drain" as experienced workers leave crucial roles. At the same time, unemployed older workers struggle to find good jobs despite unemployment rates now being at a 50-year low.

It's crazy when you think about it. The solution to your labor problems could be smack dab in plain sight, but you can't see them through the sea of gray in front of you. Could staffing your business with mature, experienced, and even retired workers become your competitive advantage?

Anti-Age Discrimination Legislation

Hiring older workers isn't just a smart business move. It's also a legal issue.

According to the U.S. Department of Labor, "The Age Discrimination in Employment Act of 1967 (ADEA) protects certain applicants and employees 40 years of age and older from discrimination on the basis of age in hiring, promotion, discharge, compensation, or terms, conditions or privileges of employment." The Equal Employment Opportunity Commission (EEOC) is responsible for enforcing this act.

Why Boomers?

Are you interested in workers motivated by stability and the opportunity to contribute their earned knowledge and skills? Loyal workers who believe in an honest day's work for an honest day's pay? Who are good at taking direction, solving problems, and going the extra mile? Who could actually mentor less-experienced employees and be a rare example of solid work ethic?

Then maybe it's time to take a look at boomers as your next source of talent.

Headquartered in the San Diego area, kW Sustainable Brands has helped hundreds of companies and employees create healthier indoor home and work environments. Kim Wallace, founder and managing partner of recruiting at kW, says, "Our brands bring eco-glam to the unglamorous world of sustainability. You need to learn from the older generation because some things you can't learn in a classroom. It's about experience. It's tough finding younger talent who have the experience required for complex projects."

Many employers I've connected with are quick to note that older workers tend to be the ones they can count on to show up early, stay late, and do a quality job. "These more experienced workers take direction well and ask questions when something isn't clear," Kim says. "In fact, they have proactively made suggestions for improvements, saving us time and money."

Jim Barnett is director of strategic intelligence analysis at the AARP. He points to several distinct advantages to hiring older employees. "These older workers bring with them valuable know-how that they have developed through years of experience," he says. "They tend to be more reliable and loyal and less likely to be chasing the next big thing. What they are looking for, by and large, is a chance to give back, make a difference, and leave a legacy. We call these 'encore careers,' where there's often a chance to pursue work that is more fulfilling, where there's challenge and perhaps an opportunity to put in place a life experience capstone."

What Is Retirement, Really?

Retirement—the practice of no longer working after a certain age—began to grow in popularity in the United States after the Industrial

Revolution (1760–1840). Life expectancy back then was only about 40 years, and people who lived long enough retired either out of choice or necessity. "Older" workers in factories, for example, were often let go or quit when they suffered from health problems that impacted their performance (e.g., slowing down assembly lines and taking sick days). Older workers were also viewed by some as holding jobs that younger workers could (and should) fill.

The concept of retirement became more widespread over the decades. President Franklin D. Roosevelt signed the Social Security Act into law in 1935, creating a federal safety net for elderly, unemployed, and disadvantaged Americans. Back in 1935, the average life expectancy was 61 years. In the United States today, it's 80 years for men and 84 years for women. As people live longer, let's just say pension systems are feeling the pressure. (The solvency of Social Security is a topic for another time.) The long and the short of it is this: then, as now, many older individuals want or need to continue working after they reach retirement age.

When it comes to basic human nature, some make the case that retirement goes against the grain. (I'll admit that I'm in the "against the grain" camp.) The idea that every individual would choose to stop working if they had adequate financial assets simply isn't true.

Think of the long list of millionaires and billionaires who say they've never once considered retiring. There's business magnate and philanthropist Warren Buffett, who's going strong in his late 80s. Rita Moreno, the famed Puerto Rican actress, dancer, and singer, has a career that has spanned more than 70 years. Music producer Quincy Jones, also in his 80s, wouldn't think of retiring. Clint Eastwood and Robert Redford are still directing (and starring in) films. Ruth Bader Ginsburg is still serving on the Supreme Court. John Williams is composing music for the upcoming Star Wars movies, and Ted Turner and Rupert Murdoch are still cutting billion-dollar business deals.

You know or have heard stories of people in perceived non-sexy jobs—janitors, waiters, dish washers, truck drivers, window washers—working years after they could have retired. The same holds true in almost every profession.

So what is retirement *really*? It's not as if people turn their brains off and start doing nothing. Instead, retirees generally do more of what they want, when they want, which gives them greater flexibility. Many take the opportunity to explore pursuits they had put on the back burner before their formal "retirement." And some make a conscious decision to return to work, turning their attention to encore careers, side hustles, and seasonal and holiday work, along with part-time, flexible, and telecommuting employment.

Why Boomers Are Going Back to Work

A survey by the RAND Corporation shows that 39 percent of employees aged 65 and older reported that they had come out of retirement.

Now, many older Americans are continuing to work or returning to work because they want the extra cash. But that's not their only motivation. Not even close. (I cover the complex subject of compensation in great depth in my book *On Fire at Work*.) Let's consider some other reasons.

Too much free time. Retirement isn't always as fun as it looks. After a few weeks, months, or years of rocking on the porch, playing a favorite sport, pursuing a long-deferred hobby, or volunteering, some retirees find they have too much free time. Single or widowed persons may not want to spend so much time alone. Or the retiree's spouse is still working.

In some cases, the retiree's spouse is also retired, and household dynamics change—not necessarily for the better. Actress Ella Harris said, "A retired husband is often a wife's full-time job." I know one guy who found it stressful to have his wife at home after she retired. "It was almost as if I was expected to entertain her all day," he told me. Not surprisingly, he encouraged her to go back to work. "I totally failed at retirement," his wife explained to me with a wink.

Routines. People often like being challenged, and they enjoy the satisfaction that comes from accomplishing tasks at work. Many may miss the routine of having somewhere to go every workday. They may also miss achieving milestones and hitting deadlines.

Social interaction. Work is in part about socializing, and the absence of regular social interaction outside the home can be a difficult adjustment for some people. Many people find friends and colleagues at work, and the transition to retirement can leave some people missing their social connections and feeling isolated and lonely.

Meaning and contribution. Boomers who retire or find their jobs phased out commonly wonder what they're going to do next. Many are looking to switch professions, change careers, or explore a hobby or a passion that they have always wanted to pursue.

The great thing is that many boomers have transferable skills, and many are taking what they've done all their lives and channeling those skills into new areas. They're looking for the right organizations and positions so they can make the best use of their expertise. And they're choosing carefully. For example, they may be seeking more purpose in their lives and demand that their work have meaning beyond simply making a profit for their employer. When older individuals choose to be employed, they often want to make a contribution, regardless of the position they hold.

World-Class Window Washer

There's a man who washes windows in Florence, South Carolina, who embodies Martin Luther King's belief that "No work is insignificant." An older gentleman, he dons a suit and tie each workday, gathers his tools—a bucket filled with water, soap, and a squeegee—and goes to work. What might seem a tedious chore for many is for him a calling. He's an artist. A performer. A professional. He's the best at what he does. And you can't help but be inspired by the extreme pride he takes in his accomplishment as he serves others through his work.

Flexible part-time or virtual employment. Some older workers value the flexibility that part-time or virtual employment offers. For example, Jean retired from a job as a home health aide at the age of 62. On the side, she had earned a certificate in processing health claims. She was enjoying a retirement lifestyle, traveling around the country with her husband in an RV and stopping at national parks and campgrounds along the way. A friend asked if she would be interested in part-time work where she could set her own hours. Jean gave it a try and found it was a good fit for her.

Health benefits. Growing evidence suggests that working longer brings health benefits. Work involves learning, social interaction, and application of cognitive skills such as problem-solving—all of which can have positive impacts on brain health. Many jobs have a physical component (also called exercise) that can keep older employees both physically fit and mentally active.

So You're Interested in Hiring a Boomer...

I hope by now you're thinking of the value and benefits you'll gain by hiring experienced workers. Below are some of your best strategies for recruitment.

Network. The top technique is to network. Who do you know— friends, neighbors, friends of friends—in the more experienced talent pool? Keep your antenna up at the places you frequent.

Partner with AARP or similar groups. AARP offers online career networking opportunities, an AARP job board, and other programs designed to help employers connect with more experienced workers. The organization also partners with community colleges and workforce organizations to help candidates 50 years and older fill in-demand jobs. In addition, the National Council on Aging offers a Senior Community Service Employment Program. A Google search will lead you to additional resources in your area.

Use online resources. Check out online resources like the SeniorJobBankSM, where you pay to post jobs through Indeed.com. You can also search for candidates using a free keyword tool.

Advertise jobs where boomers will find them. Consider advertising in the local paper. In my community, it makes sense to post jobs (with permission, of course) at the local hardware store, community center, coffee shop, and church. Decide what makes sense in your community.

Display pictures of older workers. Ensure your website photos and videos include images of more experienced team members, sending a clear message that your teams are generationally diverse.

Diversify your interview panels. For better or worse, younger hiring managers may have unconscious biases about older workers. How might a 20-something feel about hiring someone who's their grandparents' age? Address this potential problem by incorporating a variety of voices and perspectives during the interview process.

Ever Considered Launching a Returnship Program?

The Goldman Sachs Returnship Program was designed to train and mentor people who have left the workforce for two or more years and are ready to return. The ten-week program gives people an opportunity to sharpen their skills and learn new ones in a work environment that may have changed significantly since they left.

Building a Boomer-Friendly Workplace

As with other employee pools we've talked about, you can build a user-friendly workplace for older candidates. Start by valuing their experience: ask for their input about business issues, problems, and opportunities. Educate staff members about the value of leveraging the expertise of boomers. Describe to younger employees how the business (and they themselves) can benefit by asking their more experienced colleagues questions and then listening intently.

An ideal partnership could involve pairing an older worker with a younger colleague in a mutual mentorship. The older colleague has experience to offer to a younger colleague, and the younger colleague may be able to offer advice, for example, on how to become more tech-savvy.

As a boomer myself, I personally welcome the opportunity to share what I've learned over the decades...including what works and what doesn't. (In fact, I've made a career of it!)

Tips and Tactics

Boomers bring a lot to the table. They offer experience, stability, and reliability—and they can help develop and mentor younger workers. Increasingly, organizations are recognizing the benefits of hiring more experienced workers and tapping into this valuable resource. The question is this: How can employers make the work environment and the job conducive to boomers so it's a win-win?

In today's tight labor market, it's essential for smart businesses to create a climate that's attractive to older workers. The Bureau of Labor Statistics projects that those aged 55 and over will experience the fastest rates of labor force growth by 2024. Follow these tips and tactics to make sure your hiring pool includes older workers:

- Educate yourself and your staff about the value of having more experienced workers in the workplace. Give people the opportunity to show how their employment can bring value to your organization. Try not to make assumptions about skills or abilities based on age.

- Read the Age Discrimination Act of 1975 and understand the legal implications of your decisions. Ensure, for example, that you're not including age references in job descriptions and applications (e.g., asking for the year someone graduated from high school or college).

- Understand the reasons older workers and retirees want to return to work. In many cases, it's not just about a paycheck; instead, it's often about dignity, purpose, and connection.

- Post jobs and advertise open positions in local papers, shops, Bingo halls, and community centers where experienced candidates may be looking. Also network at those local spots, as well as in online spaces.

- Explore ways to make your business a boomer-friendly workplace. For example, feature workers across generations, including boomers, in work-related pictures and videos.

- Ask experienced employees advice on work improvement opportunities. Their wisdom and problem-solving abilities may lead to viable solutions that can bring you better business outcomes.

Chapter 14

WELL WORTH A SECOND CHANCE:
Hiring Ex-Offenders

After learning the systems and processes Disney uses to keep their legendary amusement parks spotlessly clean, 31-year-old Matt Peach got an idea. He figured those same skills and techniques could be applied to cleaning up large stadiums and open fields after big public events. This is what inspired Matt to create Extreme Clean, a mobile cleanup service that arrives on scene at a state fair, mega-concert, NASCAR race, or large public gathering of any kind, keep it "Disney clean" throughout the event, and then make the mess of trash and debris left behind vanish as if it never hit the ground.

Naturally, Matt and his wife, Caroline, couldn't do all the work necessary to restore hundreds of badly abused, angry acres all by themselves. They would need to find and hire dozens, if not hundreds, of temporary workers to tackle these enormous tasks. And it's not easy to find people who want to continually pick up an endless sea of trash, garbage, and disgusting waste.

However, rather than spend their precious resources on advertising these unsexy temporary job openings in the local paper, Matt and

Caroline went to jail. Not because they had done anything wrong, but because they hoped that they could tap into a source of labor that is willing to accept this kind of work.

Caroline began her search by simply calling the jails and prisons in her local area to inquire about work release programs and convict re-entry programs. She also found additional resources through faith-based programs, like Kingdom Promotions (kingdompromotions.org) and Hope for Prisoners (hopeforprisoners.org).

They hired a few prisoners and then a few more. Some had just been released and had nowhere to go. Some were living at halfway houses. Some arrived wearing ankle braces. But all appeared ready, willing, and able to work.

It didn't take Matt and Caroline long to realize that they had tapped into a massive pipeline of labor full of men and women who are chomping at the bit for a chance to get back into the workforce and prove themselves worthy of an employer's trust.

In short order, the Peaches found that hiring prisoners and ex-offenders not only made good financial sense, it also made them feel proud about the opportunities they were creating for a segment of our society that others often disregard, condemn, and pass over during the hiring process.

Curious, I had to ask Matt how many incarcerated and/or recently released offenders he has hired over the years. "A thousand. Actually, many thousands," he said.

ME: "WOW! That's way more than I thought! So how many of these offenders have turned out to be a problem for you, Matt?"

MATT: "Only one. And it wasn't a problem we couldn't deal with. The rest of them, by and large, have been incredibly hard-working, respectful, honest, and very loyal—some of the best workers you can imagine. We've hired them all over the Deep South for virtually every kind of large-scale public event you can imagine. And the prison systems are all very good about partnering with us to make this easy and convenient. You might say that prisoners and ex-offenders have been my number one labor source for years."

Matt and Caroline sold Extreme Clean several years ago, and the new owner continues to hire from jails, prisons, and halfway houses. Matt has since become an owner of a very successful automotive collision repair business. And yes, as you might suspect, Matt has once again looked to prisons to staff his auto body shop in Central Florida. Many of the men and women he's hired for his shop have been trained in collision repair and have the high-tech skills that are in high demand and short supply. I pressed him for an example of someone he's hired from prison who has been a real asset to his business.

"My shop manager was incarcerated for seven years of his life," Matt said. "And he's invaluable to me…the best body man and shop manager in the country! You know, we all make mistakes in life. It's amazing what happens when you give people a second chance. They'd work themselves to death before they'd ever disappoint you with a bad result. And because you've given them a second chance, many will come to you if their demons return. One of our guys who served time for a drug conviction approached Caroline and told her he was using again and was on a dangerous path and was afraid that he would eventually let us down. We got him into a counseling program, and he's now back on track."

A Killer Strategy for a Killer Brand

If you're into organic, non-GMO food, you've probably heard of Dave's Killer Bread, a major player in the health food market whose nutrient-rich bread products are available at supermarkets nationwide, including non-specialty grocers. But what makes Dave's Killer Bread remarkable is not just its tasty, heart-healthy products or its commitment to sustainability; it's that Dave's is also built on the core value of hiring ex-offenders—what is often referred to as "second chance employment."

Begun in Portland, Oregon, by Dave Dahl, who himself served 15 years in prison, Dave's Killer Bread operates on the principle that "hiring those who have a criminal background…gives people a second chance not only to make a living, but make a life." And they make good on this commitment: according to *Marketplace*, "a third of the company's 300 employees have a criminal past."

Hiring ex-offenders is so integral to their mission that they've created the Dave's Killer Bread Foundation, which actively combats the tendency of convicted offenders to relapse into criminal behavior by educating businesses on the benefits of employing them. The Foundation's website (Dkbfoundation.org) provides various resources for employers looking to tap into this often-overlooked labor pool, including access to:

- **the Second Chance Playbook,** free videos to help business leaders and HR specialists get started in hiring ex-offenders;

- **the Second Chance Ecosystem,** a community of recruiting partners who can help with their job search;

- **and the Second Chance Business Coalition,** a network of private sector employers with a commitment to second chance employment.

And the Dave's Killer Bread Foundation is not the only one doing important work in this arena. Mike Rowe, the host of the TV series *Dirty Jobs*, which ran for eight seasons on the Discovery Channel, created the mikeroweWORKS Foundation in 2008 to spearhead a national campaign to support skilled labor. "Our crumbling infrastructure, our widening skills gap, the disappearance of vocational education, and the strato- spheric rise in college tuition—these are not problems," Mike writes on the Foundation's website. "These are symptoms of what we value. And right now, we have to reconnect the average American with the value of a skilled workforce." To that end, the foundation's Work Ethic Scholarship Program has given more than $5 million dollars to more than 1,000 recip- ients to support more than 15 skilled trades.

Mike is a tireless advocate for opening opportunity through skill and technical training, including for ex-offenders. Here's how he makes the case in a foundation video on the Vocational Village program: "Inmates are coming back into society," he says. "Speaking selfishly, it's better for me, and it's better for you, and it's better for everybody if they're engaged and interested and on some kind of positive track." The key, as he goes on to say, is to reintroduce people to society who have useful skills and a measure of ambition or enthusiasm or hope.

As the success of Dave's Killer Bread and the organizations that benefit from the work of nonprofits like the DKB Foundation and mikeroweWORKS Foundation reveal, hiring ex-offenders is not only the right thing to do; it also just might be your competitive edge.

Should You Hire Ex-Offenders?

Vocational Village, located in Ionia, Michigan, is a program developed in 2016 that prepares adult students from across the state for in-demand jobs in skilled trades such as welding, automotive work, plumbing, and carpentry. The program combines intensive hands-on training with classroom study and life skills. Students earn state- and nationally recognized industry certifications. Vocational Village partners with employers, inviting them to the facility to view the quality of the program and to interview students as job candidates. Many trainees receive offers before they even complete the program.

By now, you've guessed that the adult students in question are in the prison system. The Vocational Village program was developed by the Michigan Department of Corrections, and students have to apply for and be accepted into the program.

Let's be clear—I'm not soft on crime. Nobody is above the law, and I firmly believe in incarcerating law breakers. With that said, I also feel that many non-violent first-time offenders can be rehabilitated and should be given a second chance. When I talk about hiring a great match for your company, that doesn't mean you have to staff your business with

Brady-like Eagle Scouts. In fact, it may be well worth your time to consider the path Matt and Caroline Peach have taken.

If someone has been convicted, has served their time, and has the right skills, knowledge, and attitude, have they earned a second chance? Depending on the nature of your business and the various positions you're trying to fill, the answer is one you may want to investigate.

To help you make that decision, allow me to share some key statistics:

- In the United States, more than 70 million people have conviction or arrest records. That's about one in three adults. Roughly 19 million adults have felony records.

- One year after being released, between 60 and 75 percent of ex-offenders don't yet have a job.

- According to research by the Society for Human Resource Management, executives in companies that have hired ex-offenders report that 82 percent of these hires have been at least as successful on the job as their average hire.

Most ex-offenders are *at least as successful* as the average hire—that's a remarkable success rate. In fact, a study of the performance of ex-convicts in the military revealed that not only were those with felony criminal backgrounds less likely to be terminated for negative reasons, but they "were also promoted faster through the ranks and more often made it to the level of sergeant than recruits who weren't offenders."

In today's economic climate, a growing number of employers of all sizes are evaluating their options when it comes to ex-offenders in the workforce. Just a few of the companies that hire ex-offenders who fit their requirements include Alamo Rent A Car, Best Western, Chili's, Comcast, Embassy Suites, Jiffy Lube, Kohl's, Landstar Trucking, Manpower, and Xerox.

Five Reasons to Hire Ex-Offenders

Here are five reasons why you might want to get ex-offenders on your radar.

1. Gratitude leads to productivity and loyalty. It can be hard for ex-offenders to find a job after they've been convicted and served their time. When an employer comes along who gives them a second chance, they tend to be extremely grateful for that job opportunity. Perhaps more importantly, they often don't want to jeopardize that opportunity at any cost.

Stephen Steurer, PhD, is an educator, criminologist, and leading expert in corrections and education. He served as executive director of the Corrections Education Association for almost 30 years and has held several other leadership positions in the area of prison education and reform, and he's a prolific researcher and author on these topics. Stephen has firsthand experience in hiring ex-offenders. "I hired ex-offenders to work at the Corrections Education Association, and they did very well," he says. He explains that employers find ex-offenders to be good hires for several reasons. "Offenders who get a second chance tend to be very dependable," he notes. "They tend to be extremely grateful for the opportunity to be employed and work hard. And they are likely to be sober since there is not supposed to be access to alcohol and drugs in prison."

In addition to showing their appreciation by coming to work on time and honoring deadlines, ex-offenders also tend to stick with the company that hired them for the long haul. If you find an ex-offender who's a good match for your company's needs and who's a capable worker, you've made an awesome hire!

2. Industry and job training. While in prison, ex-offenders may have received training specific to your industry or the jobs you need to fill. Most prison facilities offer basic literacy courses, vocational and technical training, and secondary and college-level courses. These same facilities also often establish partnerships with community colleges, four-year colleges, and workforce development organizations. Some programs provide training in food services, automotive work, cosmetology, construction, printing, roofing, and jobs in other sectors. Other programs customize training to match employers' specific requirements. Workforce development entities and unemployment offices are good places to find additional resources.

3. Tax credits. Hiring an ex-offender can also be a good business decision if your company can benefit from a tax break or a tax credit through the Internal Revenue Service's Work Opportunity Tax Credit (WOTC) program. Essentially, employers who hire eligible, unemployed ex-offenders may be eligible for a tax incentive.

4. Insurance. Employers uncertain about hiring former offenders can take advantage of a Federal Bonding Program offered by the U.S. Department of Labor that serves as a kind of insurance. Businesses that hire bond-covered ex-offenders are eligible to be reimbursed for any related losses from the first six months of employment. Many employers consider this program a "try before you buy" safety net.

5. Community well-being. When you hire a former offender, you gain a tax-paying, productive citizen who's incentivized by the dignity of work and less likely to return to crime.

Dion's Fresh Start

Dion Drew was raised in the projects in Yonkers, New York, by his mother, who worked two jobs for years to try to support the family. He started selling drugs at age 15 and was in and out of jail for 20 years. At the end of a four-year sentence in upstate New York, Dion decided to change his ways—and his life. Upon his release from prison, he set four goals for himself:

1. Get a job
2. Save some money

3. Start a family

4. Make his mom proud of him again. (This was his ultimate goal that would be achieved once his first three were reached.)

Once Dion was out of prison, he looked for work day after day, but he was routinely rejected based on his criminal record. Weeks passed, and then a friend reminded him about Greyston Bakery, a B Corp manufacturing plant that practices Open Hiring™. When a job becomes available, the company accepts the next candidate in line regardless of any criminal record or other perceived barriers such as addiction or homelessness. In other words, Greyston employs people without asking any questions about their past.

Dion signed up, and one day he got a call from Greyston asking if he wanted a job. "Absolutely!" was his immediate response. He started as an apprentice, after which time he was promoted to lead operator, then lead operator for research and development, and then supervisor.

In time, Dion accomplished all four of his goals. He got a job—and a great one at that. His job provided health insurance, dental insurance, and life insurance, three things he had for the first time in his life. He started a family and has since opened three bank accounts, one of which is dedicated to saving for his daughter's future. Best of all? His mom now calls Dion at least twice a week to let him know how proud she is of him.

Mike Brady, Greyston President and CEO, says Dion represents success and leadership in the 21st century and explains that Greyston has been effectively using their open hiring model since 1982. This model focuses on the whole person in employment instead of screening based on job requirements and performance measurements.

Greyston makes it a priority to support each employee and eliminate challenges to success on the job. All employees work with team members who help them define goals for career and life. The company then identifies appropriate levels of support, including training, childcare, and safe housing. Mike emphasizes that the more than 2,000 people whom Greyston has hired have put more than $18 million back into the challenged economy of southwest Yonkers.

Second Chance Hires— What Employers Should Know

Ban the Box?

TRUE OR FALSE: Your job applications should include a checkbox as to whether the candidate has a criminal record.

ANSWER: Maybe. A growing number of states, counties, and cities have passed "ban the box" legislation.[8] In these states, it's illegal to include a "convictions check" on an application. The primary rationale behind these laws is to reduce recidivism rates (the number of released felons returning to prison). If ex-offenders have a job, the thinking goes, they're less likely to commit a crime.

Many ex-offenders have struggled to be hired in the past. Part of being an employer of choice means having an effective, streamlined application process that attracts eligible candidates. It's important to recognize that a "convictions" checkbox can discourage potential hires from applying, as they may assume they won't be considered. In today's tight job market, some employers are giving ex-offenders another look, voluntarily removing questions about criminal offenses from applications.

When Can You Ask About Criminal Convictions?

You *can* ask about criminal records when you're ready to make a job offer. This is true in all states. However, the ban in some states makes it illegal to ask about convictions before you plan to make an offer. Regardless, when you're ready to offer a job you can still conduct a background check.

---

8   Note: The laws in states are different and can change, so check the laws in your area.

When Should You Reject a Candidate Because of a Criminal Record?

The answer here also depends on the situation and should likely consider the relationship of the criminal offense to the responsibilities of the job you're hiring for. If you run a preschool or daycare center, for example, you *cannot* hire convicted child sexual abuse offenders. That should really go without saying.

Other areas can be more subjective. Two questions to consider:

1. **Does the conviction relate to the job?** You might reject a convicted bank robber from working as a bank teller with access to cash. You might hire that person, however, to be part of a cleaning or landscaping crew.

2. **How long ago was the conviction?** If an ex-offender has had a clean record for a long time (say, two decades), that length of time may be worth considering as a factor in a hiring decision.

Should You Tell Your Workforce about the New Hire's Criminal Record?

Many experts advise that criminal records should be shared on a "need to know" basis. For example, HR and relevant business leaders should probably know, but team members on the floor or in the field might not necessarily need that information. So what should you do if you don't share information and other employees find out through a Google search or other means? A best practice may be to make it clear to employees that all candidates, including those with records, are considered for employment.

This Is What Equal Employment Opportunity Looks Like...

The U.S. Equal Employment Opportunity Commission (EEOC) requires you to give candidates a chance to explain their particular circumstances regarding any identified criminal offense if you determine that a criminal record makes those candidates unqualified for a job.

Be sure to treat people of different genders and races the same when it comes to hiring. You're probably not EEOC compliant if you hire a woman with a drug conviction that occurred ten years earlier but reject a man with the same job qualifications who has a similar criminal record.

Naturally, there are gray areas when it comes to this domain and variances in law from state to state and even locality to locality. Please consult an employment lawyer if you're planning to reject a candidate because of a conviction or if you're uncertain as to the best legal course of action.

Tips and Tactics

You may find that some ex-offenders would make an excellent fit for your company's needs. You may also find that the right candidates will stick with your company for the long haul and work to show you each and every day that they won't jeopardize the opportunity you've given them. Consider these strategies for hiring success:

- Do your homework. Call the jails and prisons in your area and ask about their work release programs and re-entry programs. Get to know the facts. See if this is a labor source that could work out for your business.

- Consider removing the "criminal checkbox" from your company's job applications. (Regardless, review the "ban the box" laws in your state and local area.)

- Try to avoid stereotypes associated with people who hold criminal records. Use an open hiring model that focuses on the whole person. When evaluating candidates for open positions, get to know the whole person first.

- Ensure the process for hiring and developing ex-offenders follows the same standard and rigor as that for other employees.

- Determine if candidates have received training specific to your industry or the jobs you need to fill. Such training could increase those candidates' value to your organization.

- Take advantage of a Federal Bonding Program offered by the U.S. Department of Labor that serves as a kind of insurance.

- Take advantage of tax breaks or tax credits through the Internal Revenue Service's WOTC program, if possible.

Chapter 15

AMERICANS WITH DISABILITIES:
A Goldmine of Potential

Randy Lewis, a former vice president at Walgreens, led a division with 10,000 employees and hired 1,000 new people each year. He wanted to demonstrate to the world that employees with disabilities can perform as well—or better—than their peers. His motivation, in part, came from his son, Austin, who was diagnosed with autism at the age of three. Randy recognized that he and others constantly underestimated what Austin could accomplish. (As just one example, Austin passed his driver's license test on the first try.)

In 2007, Walgreens completed a new distribution center in Anderson, South Carolina. Randy set the following goal: persons with disabilities would make up one-third of the Anderson workforce. All employees would earn equal pay for equal work and be held to the same standards. When Randy presented the plan to the board of directors, one member asked, "What if it doesn't work?" As with any business initiative, Randy said they would give it their best shot, evaluate, and adjust.

Word got out about the plan, which garnered a great deal of media attention. In fact, some job candidates from across the country moved to South Carolina for a chance to work at the center.

Desiree was one of these candidates who relocated in pursuit of meaningful work. Previously a temporary employee in San Diego, she had a rare muscle disease that made it difficult to walk. One day she showed up to work with a walker, and her boss told her to come back when she didn't need assistance. Desiree moved her family from California to South Carolina to work at the Walgreens distribution center, where she became a successful supervisor.

Angie has cerebral palsy. She earned all A's as an undergraduate at Clemson University and all A's in graduate school. Upon graduation, she sent out 300 résumés and went to 30 interviews. She didn't receive a single job offer. Angie was subsequently hired at the Walgreens distribution center in South Carolina, where she became one of the best HR managers in the entire company.

Harrison has autism. During his Walgreens interview, Harrison told Randy that he could process 60 cases of goods an hour. Randy replied that the distribution center standard was 40 cases per hour. Randy hired Harrison, who did indeed perform at 150 percent of the distribution center standard. Harrison also succeeded at every other task he was assigned. Randy notes that Harrison, a star employee, would have slipped through the cracks at many organizations if he had gone through a regular hiring process.

Once the distribution center was up and running, Randy's team began evaluating the center's performance as a potential model for Walgreens and other companies. After extensive studies that covered 400,000 employee working hours, the results were in: people with disabilities performed as well or better than their peers. Employees with disabilities had better safety records, higher retention rates, less absenteeism, and fewer workers' comp claims. The bottom line: the Anderson facility turned out to be the most productive center in the history of the company.

Walgreens rolled out the model across other distribution centers. The company also shared their plan, process, and research with business leaders from hundreds of companies of all sizes, and many companies have since launched initiatives adapting what they have learned. The National Governors Association has called it the "gold standard of disability employment."

Today, Randy runs NOGWOG (which stands for No Greatness Without Goodness), a nonprofit organization that helps companies build successful hiring programs for people with disabilities.

The Americans with Disabilities Act

On a bright summer day in 1990, President George H. W. Bush stood at a podium in the White House Rose Garden to sign the Americans with Disabilities Act (ADA). He heralded the act as the world's first "comprehensive declaration of equality for people with disabilities," as well as the start of a new civil rights era in America.

In his remarks, President Bush noted that the key to successful implementation of the ADA rests in large part with the business community. He said, "This act does something important for American business—and remember this: You've called for new sources of workers. Well, many of our fellow citizens with disabilities are unemployed. They want to work, and they can work.... And remember, this is a tremendous pool of people who will bring to jobs diversity, loyalty, proven low turnover rate, and only one request: the chance to prove themselves."

The ADA states that a person with a disability is someone who has a mental or physical impairment that limits one or more major activities in life. According to the U.S. Census Bureau, more than 40 million people in the United States have some form of disability. In today's tight labor market, persons with disabilities can be a great source of talent. And yet here's a sobering statistic: the Bureau of Labor Statistics says that in 2018 the unemployment rate for people with a disability was 8 percent, more than twice the rate for those with no disability.

Decades after the ADA was signed into law, many employers still don't understand the benefits of hiring candidates with disabilities, and many persons with disabilities still don't know how to find the jobs they're seeking.

Ten Reasons to Hire People with Disabilities

The National Center on Health, Physical Activity and Disability created an inspiring, funny video starring high school student Mary White, host of *The Awesome Mary Show*. Mary was born with cerebral palsy and hydrocephalus, a condition that has caused her to undergo 36 neurosurgeries. In the video, "Mary's Top 10: Hiring People with a Disability," Mary shares ten reasons to hire this largely untapped source of talent:

1. **Hiring people with disabilities creates a more positive workspace.**

2. **Accommodations can be more affordable than you think.** As Mary says, "Sometimes [accommodations] cost less than those free snacks in the grocery store. That's zero, zip, zilch, nothing!"

3. **Workers with disabilities are highly motivated, are dependable, and have great attendance records.** Mary states enthusiastically, "If you give me a task, I'm going to do it. I love to work!"

4. **Many times workers with disabilities have significant support systems in place**, along with job coaches from public and private organizations, to help them stay successful in the workplace.

5. **People with disabilities can bring fresh and diverse perspectives to work teams.**

6. **Businesses can take advantage of a great PR and business opportunity.** Mary points out that people with disabilities and their friends and families add up to a trillion-dollar market.

7. **Employers can gain great new employees in today's tough job market.** Mary stresses that your hard-to-fill job just might match her superpower! (She also emphasizes the importance of equal pay for equal work.)

8. **People with disabilities tend to be good at following rules**, which is why they're less likely to get hurt at work.

9. **Uncle Sam offers financial incentives to employers who hire people with disabilities.**

10. **The best person for the job may well be a person with a disability**. "Forget all this fuss," Mary says, "and just hire us!"

Over the decades, substantial research has supported Mary's arguments (and President Bush's claims that employers who hire people with disabilities experience positive business results). The U.S. Department of Labor reports a 90 percent increase in retention, 72 percent increase in employee productivity, and 45 percent increase in safety at work. A study by Accenture and the American Association of People with Disabilities also found the following additional financial returns for companies that actively strive to hire people with disabilities compared to those that don't:

- Revenues were 28 percent higher.

- Net incomes were twice as high.

- Profit margins were 30 percent higher.

Simply put, hiring people with disabilities makes good business sense.

Barriers to Hiring

In spite of all the evidence of the positive impact of hiring persons with disabilities, many employers are reluctant to actively recruit candidates from this talent pool. Three of the primary barriers are not knowing (1) how to make accommodations, (2) where to find candidates, and (3) how to create an inclusive workplace. Below, I'll share some strategies to address these barriers.

Making Accommodations

ADA nondiscrimination standards stipulate that employers with 15 or more workers are required to provide "reasonable accommodations" to enable a person with a disability who is qualified for a position to perform essential job functions.

Some employers believe they'll need to invest heavily to meet this requirement. However, a survey conducted under a U.S. Department of Labor contract found that 59 percent of reasonable accommodations cost nothing and others average about $500. Examples of reasonable accommodations include the following:

- Improving workspace accessibility
- Allowing flexible work schedules
- Making adjustments to equipment
- Providing specialized software
- Allowing service animals at work
- Providing relevant training
- Helping with transportation
- Reserving convenient parking spaces

As noted above, an inclusive workplace offers clear advantages to your organization, and investment in reasonable accommodations often brings high returns. (To learn more about ADA compliance, check out the Job Accommodation Network, which offers free consultation, services, and resources for employers of all sizes.)

Connecting with Candidates Who Have Disabilities

Many employers don't know how to find or connect with people with disabilities. That's where workforce development organizations come in. In addition to networking and referrals, some organizations specialize in helping companies recruit and hire persons with disabilities. For example, Randy Lewis from Walgreens reached out to a South Carolina agency that supported his hiring initiatives. The agency invested time into understanding the positions available, pre-screened candidates, and provided job coaching to help transition employees into their new positions.

Numerous organizations are dedicated to matching people with disabilities with employers, so find what's working in your area. To get you started, I'll highlight a few examples below.

Vocational rehabilitation agencies. Every state has a vocational rehabilitation agency dedicated to helping people with mental or physical disabilities obtain, maintain, or return to employment. These agencies offer no-cost services that connect employers to qualified candidates. They also offer tax credits and other financial incentives to employers that hire people with disabilities. In addition, the agencies can help cover costs associated with special training, equipment, and other accommodations and support. (The Job Accommodation Network is a key resource for information about state vocational rehabilitation agencies.)

Employer Assistance and Resource Network on Disability Inclusion (EARN). Funded by the U.S. Department of Labor's Office of Disability Employment Policy, EARN is a free resource that provides information and assistance to employers in such areas as recruitment and hiring, retention, advancement, workplace accessibility, laws and regulations, and federal contractor requirements. Employers can access free webinars and training videos.

Disability:IN (DisabilityIN.org). This major nonprofit organization is a network of business leadership network affiliates that help companies identify best practices in hiring and retaining people with disabilities and building inclusive corporate cultures.

Centers for independent living. Centers for independent living are community-based, cross-disability nonprofit agencies designed and operated within local communities by people with disabilities. The centers provide a variety of services that promote independent living for people with disabilities. Contact a local center for help with hiring—many offer pre-employment services.

Online resources. Many websites connect employers with candidates with disabilities, including the American Association for People with Disabilities (AAPD.com), AbilityJobFair.org, and GettingHired.com.

Creating an Inclusive Workplace Environment

Creating an inclusive environment is a critical part of being a great employer. The tips below apply to people with disabilities but also cover the wants and needs of many of your employees.

Focus on ability and don't make assumptions. Stereotypes of people with disabilities are often based on assumptions made about those individuals' limitations. Randy Lewis says that among the many barriers to employment, "the unkindest cut of all is that 99.99 percent of us believe that a person with a disability can't do the job as well." Focus on ability, not disability—focus on what each person *can* do.

People with disabilities have learned to navigate everyday demands, so make the most of the skills they've built throughout their lives. It's likely that those who have had difficulty with their hearing or sight, for instance, have learned strategies for making the workplace more accessible, friendlier, and safer for them. Along those lines, rather than creating your own workarounds to address someone's needs, involve them in the process and ask them to share their thoughts. Their real-world insights may far surpass your makeshift attempts at accommodating their needs.

Broaden your candidate screening process. People with disabilities may or may not have a job record, and they may or may not be able to ace an interview. Open the door by giving candidates a chance to demonstrate their capabilities. You can also partner with organizations that have established processes for finding and screening candidates for your open positions.

Make reasonable accommodations in advance. If possible, put accommodations in place before a person with a disability starts the job. For instance, if you're planning to hire a blind employee, make the work area accessible and install a braille program on the candidate's computer.

Be flexible. Some situations simply aren't covered in the employee manual and may require sound judgment. One employee with autism in a stockroom loved the color orange and would clap every time he saw an orange product. The manager asked the other employees about the behavior, and they agreed that they preferred clapping to complaining. The consensus: "He's one of the team."

Integrate employees with disabilities into your team. Involve persons with disabilities in meetings, decisions, breaks, and celebrations. I spoke with one employee with disabilities who said he had been ignored at school and felt extremely lonely. That all changed when he was hired at a company with an inclusive workplace environment. Now he loves going to work each day and enjoys spending time with his co-workers, who have become his friends.

Show respect. Tolerate absolutely no harassment or bullying. Your organization should have a strict harassment policy in place, along with a process for enforcing it.

Set everyone up for success. The goal should be to treat all employees the same. Some employees—including some with disabilities—can benefit from extra effort and training to ensure they clearly understand company rules and expectations. Once employees are onboarded and trained, expect quality work. Hold all employees to the same standard for work performance and recognize accomplishments. (And remember—equal pay for equal work. Hopefully this one's a no-brainer.)

HIRING THE HOMELESS?

Job candidates with disabilities might face another level of hiring bias if they are homeless. However, companies can and do benefit from recognizing the employment potential in both groups.

John Everett, general manager at the renowned Westin in downtown Denver, is experiencing fantastic results with hiring through the Back on My Feet program. Now operating in 13 major US cities, this privately funded nonprofit helps the homeless transition back into the workforce by training people who've experienced incredibly difficult times to run marathons. Program participants develop the strength, confidence, and self-esteem to overcome their challenges, and that's just the start of it. More than 6,500 BOMF members have been trained with the in-demand hard skills and key soft skills to become attractive job candidates for employers.

Everett, an avid runner, told me that the people who've been through the Back on My Feet program emerge ready and willing to go the extra mile in tackling the toughest jobs and are so grateful for the opportunities they are given.

Tips and Tactics

Many employers find that having employees with disabilities on the team drives a positive, people-oriented—versus exclusively process-oriented—culture. People of all descriptions who have traditionally been underestimated can become valuable contributors when their companies and peers make sure that their talents are recognized and their voices are heard. Consider these strategies as part of your company's recruitment and hiring plan:

- Recognize that the ADA prohibits employers from discriminating against applicants and workers in all aspects of employment. Understand your responsibility in providing reasonable accommodations.

- Review the research about the business benefits of hiring workers with disabilities. Consider the value of a job for the person in question in terms of their independence, confidence, and connections at work.

- Develop a culture that is inclusive to employees with disabilities (and for every employee).

- Become familiar with resources that can help you develop strategies to connect with candidates with disabilities. If appropriate, focus on candidates' abilities to perform a job (versus basing decisions only on employment history, assessments, and interviewing skills).

- Take advantage of tax incentives and other support that you may be eligible to receive when you hire employees with disabilities.

- Brainstorm a variety of ways in which people with disabilities can demonstrate their ability to do a job. They may be a perfect fit for the position in question, but for a fair evaluation you need to be able to define the job in terms of its essential tasks. In developing a detailed understanding of what a job requires, you also may discover that accommodating employees' needs isn't that difficult (or expensive).

PART 3

KEEPING GREAT EMPLOYEES

Chapter 16

PERFECTING YOUR HIRING FUNNEL
Assessing, Interviewing, & Tracking Candidates

p to 95 percent of companies report they have made poor hiring decisions, and up to 80 percent of turnover results from poor hiring decisions.

I hire based on gut instinct. Let's just say it's not working out as well as I had hoped.

I say "yes" a lot more in today's world because you can't be choosy in this labor market.

I no longer interview applicants. It's like they're interviewing me as I try to sell them on working here!

If applicants show up on time for the interview, I like 'em. And if I like 'em, I hire 'em. Strangely, though, they don't always show up on time for work once they're hired…

> Something weird happened! Although their DNA was identical, the person I interviewed and hired was not the same person who reported for the job. It's like I was duped.

These are just a few of the things I've heard from the thousands of business owners and managers I've talked to over the years. Hiring is a mysterious process that's hard to pin down. Employers are winging it. They're relying on instinct, doing the best they can, hiring anyone available, and hoping that their new employees show up on time (or at all) and do the jobs they've been hired to do.

Like many of these employers, maybe you feel you don't know how to get off the hire/train/turnover treadmill. Maybe you complain to family and friends. Maybe you make jokes at parties about your hiring pool and revolving door of employees. But deep inside you know it's not funny. Deep inside, you're frustrated. Grudgingly, you accept that this hiring nightmare is just something you have to contend with.

But it doesn't have to be this way.

Research shows that gut instinct alone isn't a reliable predictor of successful performance or job retention. Including more objective steps in your hiring process will lead to better candidate–job matches, which in turn will have a huge impact on your business.

Poor Hiring Decisions Are the Bane of Your Business Existence

According to *Harvard Business Review* data, up to 80 percent of turnover is caused by poor hiring decisions. If you're among those who believe you could do a better job with employee selection, you're not alone. In a *CareerBuilder* survey, almost three-quarters (74 percent) say they've hired a person who is a poor match for a job. Brandon-Hall research has that number at 95 percent.

As I've mentioned, Craig Lamb of Rowan-Cabarrus Community College in North Carolina has a proven record of helping employers of all sizes recruit and retain employees. Regarding the hiring practices he has seen over decades in the field, Craig observes: "Most companies wouldn't let a product come into a building without an inspection process that ensures it is the right product and the quantity and quality that was ordered. Yet many employers hire workers without any process at all."

Craig shares this analogy about matching candidates to jobs: "Imagine if a football team hired [New England Patriots quarterback] Tom Brady and put him in the game as a defensive end. Then after a probation period, they let him go based on poor performance on the job. There's real value in determining up front whether you have a good match between a candidate and a position. It really is common sense."

Perfecting Your Hiring Funnel

If you've ever worked in sales, you're familiar with the "sales funnel." Essentially, companies funnel a broad set of interested leads into a narrower set of buying customers. A hiring funnel might follow the same general principles.

To hire the right people, you'll need to interact with a lot of potential applicants. However, because you've built a great place to work, you're not going to allow just anyone to enter your hiring funnel. Qualified applicants are looking to work for a company like yours. They're specifically searching for the job you're looking to fill. Your first order of business is to weed out anyone who's unqualified.

Now, I know what you're thinking: "In today's labor market, I can't afford to weed out anyone!" Let me remind you that your staff shortage is only part of your problem. Hiring the wrong people for the wrong jobs and then watching those people wave goodbye after you've invested in them is the other part.

Your ability to be FULLY STAFFED is directly related to your ability to attract as many qualified applicants as possible, which is why this chapter is preceded by a dozen chapters on recruiting tactics. If you've truly built a great place to work and you've followed the strategies outlined in the book, then you will eventually be in a position where you can pick and choose. What you'll need then is a process for separating the wheat from the chaff or, to put it bluntly, the winners from the losers.

To recap, only qualified applicants will enter your hiring funnel. You'll nurture those applicants through the funnel with a process of education and awareness (you're learning about them as they're learning about you), interest (you're each determining if you want to go steady), and action (let's do this thing!). Along the way, you'll eliminate from the prospect pool anyone who, upon closer analysis, doesn't seem to be the right fit.

Of course, the more prospects that remain in your funnel, the better your odds of converting them into employees. It's all a numbers game—you need large numbers of qualified applicants at the top of your funnel if you want to increase the actual number of qualified applicants that emerge out of the much smaller opening at the bottom of the funnel.

If you want to hire three "right fits," you may need 30 people to apply. Of those 30, you'd be way ahead of the pack if you choose 20 to take an online assessment. Of those, you might feel that 15 are worthy of an interview. Of those 15 interviewed, it would be astounding if you liked 10 enough to invest in doing background checks. Let's say that 6 of those applicants pass the background check, and you offer all 6 a job. Three of those who meet your right-fit criteria may accept your offer—but, as you know, that doesn't necessarily mean that all 3 will actually report on the first day.

You can see why you need to increase your applicant flow—and why that applicant flow should include as many qualified applicants as possible. However, not all applicants should make it to your funnel.

Recruiting delivery drivers for three major Anheuser-Busch distributors in Oklahoma, Carrie Corbin realized how many applicants came through her doors thinking that being the "Bud Guy" was the fun and sexy job that was portrayed on Budweiser's popular television commercials. Seeing the line out the door of these prospective candidates and knowing that only a handful were actually capable of the physicality of the jobs she was looking to fill, Carrie decided to give each candidate a quick swim in the sea of reality. She'd simply tell them to look through the window at the large truck in the parking lot as she told each candidate that those massive vehicles had to be loaded and unloaded each day. She would then ask each candidate how they felt about carrying around armfuls of 25-pound dumbbells every day, all day. "A lot of our applicants would immediately self-deselect," Carrie said.

The moral? Don't let everyone who applies into your hiring funnel.

While there is no one right way for all employers to process applicants, there is definitely a way that is best for your business. This chapter examines one very commonly used process with several key filters to make sure the right hires flow through the funnel and become part of your organization.

The primary goal of your hiring funnel (and you have one whether or not you choose to look at it as a funnel) should be to generate a consistent base of prospective employees by cracking the applicant-to-employee code. If your company is a large and recognized brand, applicants will know about you but may not understand why they should work for you. If your company is smaller and less well known, applicants may not even know you exist. But regardless of your company's size or the sexiness of the jobs you are trying to fill, do everything in your power to bring qualified applicants into your funnel, then cultivate those applicants, and hire only the ones who are a strong fit for your organization and your open positions.

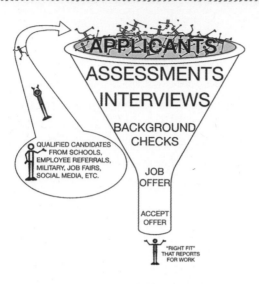

ASSESSMENTS

INTERVIEWS

BACKGROUND CHECKS

QUALIFIED CANDIDATES FROM SCHOOLS, EMPLOYEE REFERRALS, MILITARY, JOB FAIRS, SOCIAL MEDIA, ETC.

JOB OFFER

ACCEPT OFFER

"RIGHT FIT" THAT REPORTS FOR WORK

Assessments

Because hiring can be more of a subjective than an objective process, using assessments can lead to better candidate–job matches. In the past, assessments were used primarily for executive and mid-level positions. Today they're also commonly used with candidates for hourly and entry-level jobs. Experts estimate that 70 percent of employers use assessments to help answer the question: Does the candidate have the skills, abilities, and attitudes needed to perform on the job?

The three most common assessment types are personality assessments, skill assessments, and behavioral assessments. In addition to providing a key factor in hiring decisions, assessments can be the foundation for onboarding and development if candidates are hired.

Note that assessments in hiring are meant to discriminate, but the goal is to discriminate fairly. Testing as a factor in hiring is legal so long as an appropriately developed employment assessment is administered in line with its intended purpose. Tasks and topics on the assessment should relate to the job. (That's another reason why defining the job requirements and responsibilities is crucial.)

Personality assessments. Employers often say that they can teach the technical aspects of a job, which is why they're looking for soft skills and core values like attitude, initiative, and respect above all else. Personality assessments identify a candidate's tendencies related to their personality.

Start by recognizing that there is no good or bad, strong or weak, or right or wrong when it comes to personality. What matters is whether a person's personality is a good fit for the job and company culture.

Also recognize that people sometimes adapt their behavior and develop skills to optimize a particular personality trait. For example, an extrovert may have learned that they're more effective if they listen well in meetings and take into account others' views in decision-making. As another example, some worriers may find ways to channel fears and concerns into productivity.

Skills assessments. These assess a range of technical skills, such as mechanical ability, verbal and numerical reasoning, and software proficiency. These objective questions have absolute right and wrong responses to show whether candidates have the skills needed to do a specific job. In addition, they can reveal what skills candidates need to learn. (Skills building can become part of their development plan.)

Behavioral assessments. A behavioral assessment can reveal a candidate's work ethic, reliability, and even honesty. TraitSet is one well-known vendor for behavioral assessments and screening tools targeted primarily to frontline or hourly employees.

Interviews

Without question, the job interview is the most important part of the hiring process. The interview is where you'll invest the majority of your time and resources into selecting the right people. The managers who get the best results are the ones who take time to prepare, know how to set the right tone, and use carefully crafted questions with an understanding of what type of responses they're seeking.

The Face-to-Face Interview Sets the Tone for the Employer/Employee Relationship

Clayton Houston is the senior manager and recruiting coordinator for the Lally Group, which owns and operates seven Two Men and a Truck franchises in Cincinnati and Northern Kentucky. Collectively, they employ more than 220 frontline movers and do more than $17 million in business each year. Clayton's job is to keep those seven individual franchise operators fully staffed with strong, reliable, capable workers.

Here's how Clayton describes his organization's hiring funnel and interview process:

We aren't fly-by-night movers who show up late. We're a classy operation, and we go out of our way to show up to our customers' homes with professional-looking movers. Finding and keeping those kinds of men and women is no easy task, but our entire business depends on it.

We keep our hiring funnel filled by capitalizing on what makes us different from our competitors, such as our close-knit culture. We cast a broad net and interview selectively. We post accurate job descriptions and clearly communicate our expectations to weed out those who can't cut the mustard. We don't want to clog our funnel with people who aren't right for us. We know that it takes about ten people in the top of our funnel to generate one really good fit that we end up hiring.

We believe in the face-to-face interview. And it is up to us, the hiring managers, to set the tone for success. When an applicant comes in for an interview, we jump out of our seat, warmly welcome them, and shake their hand. We make certain our body language signals to that applicant that we are excited about what we do and that we are excited about the possibility of their joining our team. We take time to hear their story—and everyone has a story. That opens the door to tell them ours.

Our story explains how we got to be of the largest multi-unit owners of the renowned Two Men and a Truck brand. We make certain every applicant knows that we are a tight family with lofty goals for our company, and we only hire people who share those lofty goals and want to be part of a family like ours. We're not just going to hire a guy simply because he can pass a drug screen. Our interview questions have been carefully crafted to enable us to filter out those who aren't right for us. We work hard to get this part right, so we hire people who are going to be with us for the long term.

First things first: what *NOT* to ask in an interview. Everyone involved in interviewing must be aware of the questions they must not ask during an interview. The law is clear that you may not ask any question that could discriminate against a candidate. Asking questions, for example, about race, religion, gender, or other legally protected characteristics could lead to a potential lawsuit or investigation based on a candidate's complaint to the U.S. Equal Employment Opportunity Commission (EEOC).

Like Clayton Houston, many employers have told me that they like to talk about their company's family atmosphere during interviews to show that they care about their people. However, there's a fine line between what you can and cannot ask about the applicant's family, among other topics. Before venturing down a bumpy road, know the legal implications and proceed with extreme caution.

Based on EEOC guidelines, you should steer clear of any questions regarding an applicant's:

- race, color, or national origin
- religion or spiritual beliefs
- sex, gender identity, or sexual orientation
- pregnancy status
- disability
- age or genetic information
- citizenship
- marital status or number of children

The table on the next page provides a few examples of acceptable and unacceptable questions.

Acceptable and Unacceptable Inquiries for Interviews and Employment Applications

Topic	Acceptable	Unacceptable	If Unacceptable, What Is the Reason?
Age	If age is a legal requirement (for example, to be truck driver), you can ask, "If hired, can you furnish proof of age?" or state that hiring is subject to age verification.	What is your date of birth?	Could be viewed as age discrimination
Attendance and Reliability	Do you have responsibilities other than work that will interfere with specific job requirements such as traveling?	What are your childcare arrangements?	Could be viewed as discriminatory toward females
Citizenship/ National Origin	Are you legally eligible for employment in the United States?	What is your national origin? Where are your parents from?	Could be considered national origin discrimination
Disabilities	Can you perform the duties of the job you are applying for?	Do you have any disabilities?	Could be considered discrimination against people with disabilities
Language	What languages do you speak and write fluently? (ask only if the job requires additional languages)	What is your native language? How did you learn to read, write or speak English?	Could be considered national origin discrimination
Gender	Acceptable only if there is a bona fide occupational qualification	Do you wish to be addressed as Mr., Mrs., Miss, or Ms.?	Could be considered gender discrimination
Education	Do you have a high school diploma or equivalent? Do you have a university or college degree? (ask if relevant to job performance)	What year did you graduate from high school or college?	Could be considered age discrimination

Source: Society for Human Resources Management (SHRM)

Dating before saying your "I do's." Ideally, an interview should reveal how a candidate thinks, how and what they value and prioritize, what kinds of demands or expectations they're bringing to the workplace, and any useful talents or skills they possess that they haven't told you about or clarified in depth. An effective interview should also reveal any deficiencies or weaknesses that can limit the candidate's job performance or make them a bad fit for your organization's culture.

Think about it this way: you'd really want to get to know someone before you got married. Consider the job interview (or interviews) as your chance to "date" your candidate before exchanging vows (a.k.a., mutually satisfying long-term employment). If you don't want this new employer-employee relationship to end up in a quick or, worse, ugly divorce, you must take every precaution to make sure it's a great match for both your organization and the candidate. The interview is the best tool you have in your arsenal to determine if this relationship is going to work.

Open interviews. Scott Ramsey is an area manager for Office Pride, a commercial cleaning company with franchise operations in hundreds of North American cities. As you might imagine, it's difficult for Scott to find and keep good people who are eager to clean offices during evening hours. For some candidates, it's also difficult to jump through a drawn-out process to get hired for these hard-to-fill jobs.

Scott uses paid Craigslist ads to inform area job seekers that Office Pride is holding open interviews on Wednesday afternoons between 12:30 and 3:30. To appeal to his ideal candidates, he lets them know that to apply, all they need to do is show up during those hours and fill out minimal paperwork. No hassle. No hoops. Scott's Office Pride region has had as many as 15 people show up on Wednesday afternoons, and he has found a lot of great workers this way.

Behavioral interviews. Past workplace behavior is the best predictor for future on-the-job performance. Behavioral interviews are powerful because they're designed to evaluate a candidate's fit for a job by asking them about their previous workplace experiences and behavior—or in the case of first-job applicants, their performance in school. One thing that makes behavioral interviews so effective is that all candidates for a position are asked the same questions, treated the same throughout the interview process, and evaluated based on the same "scorecard." The candidate has the opportunity to demonstrate their potential for succeeding in a new position by describing how they handled similar situations in the past.

Behavioral interview questions should be based on job-related competencies, with the applicant being evaluated using the same rating scale and guidelines for acceptable answers.

Here's a basic process for preparing for a behavioral interview:

1. Identify the specific competencies needed for the job you're hiring for. For example, it might not make sense to ask a candidate applying for a position as a supermarket clerk how they used persuasive communication to solve a problem in their recent job as a pizza delivery driver, but it would be helpful to know how they managed to meet stressful deadlines, especially when a co-worker let them down or a customer expressed frustration over a late delivery.

2. Select 3–5 competencies you would like to ask questions about. It's better to go deep with a few key competencies than to ask shallow questions that don't really help you evaluate the candidate. (In other words, don't ask, "If you could be a tree, what kind of tree would you be?")

3. Stay away from yes–no questions. Rather than ask, "Do you have a strong work ethic?" ask: "Tell me about a time your workday ended before you were able to finish an important task."

4. Create (or fine-tune) a rating system and make it as objective as possible. What keywords and replies will tell you that this candidate is a match, and which will signal to you that this candidate isn't a good match for this job or your culture?

A popular and effective way to ask questions and evaluate responses during a behavioral interview is the STAR method. This format takes the interview down a predetermined path where the candidate answers questions related to a specific Situation, Task, Action they took, and Results of that action.

Here's a STAR method interview example:

Q: Tell me about a time at work when you saw someone do something dishonest. (SITUATION)

A: I saw this co-worker at my last job pocket $20 from the register.

Q: What was the policy the store had in place if you saw a co-worker stealing? (TASK)

A: We were told to report theft immediately to our department manager or HR.

Q: What did you do when the theft happened? (ACTION)

A: It was my manager's day off and HR was closed for the night, so I reported it to store security.

Q: How did that end up? (RESULT)

A: The guy got fired, but he didn't know I turned him in. I got a nice compliment from my manager.

Your organization may have a competency model or job description that includes attributes that you want to ask about during the interview. Select two or three areas and then develop—or google and find—questions to ask. A few examples are given in the table on the next page.

Competency	Questions
Initiative	Tell me about a time when you put in extra effort at work to complete a task or achieve a goal.
Problem-Solving	Tell me about a time when you had to solve a problem or work through an unanticipated situation at work.
Teamwork	Tell me about a time when you had to solve a difficult situation with a person at work.
Resilience (Coping with Pressures and Setbacks)	Tell me about a time when you had to perform under pressure at work.
Adaptability	Tell me about at time when there was a lot of change at work. How did you adapt?
Communication	Tell me about a time when you used persuasion at work to complete a task.

Keep copious notes. Employers should take notes during the interview to document their findings and create a record of the hiring process. While taking notes, the interviewer should maintain eye contact as much as possible and create a positive atmosphere for the candidate. In addition, the interviewer should focus and take notes on the *candidate's responses* (not on the candidate).

Applicant Tracking

The hiring process is a two-way street. While you're evaluating candidates, they're evaluating your company. From the moment you contact candidates through the assessments, interviews, background checks, and job offer, you have an opportunity to demonstrate how your company values and treats its employees.

You never get a second chance to make a first impression, and the people you hire, along with those you don't hire, will form an instant impression of your organization. Impressions can make or break the reputation of your workplace culture. To establish and maintain a reputation as a great place to work, you must treat every applicant with the same care and consideration as you would a cherished customer. And that begins with the speed with which you respond.

In today's competitive labor market, it's not necessarily the big companies that recruit all the good people; instead, it's the fast ones that eat the slow ones for breakfast. Have you ever reviewed an application you received days earlier and thought, "Wow! This person is a PERFECT match for us!" only to discover that your perfect match had already taken another job with your competitor? Then you know why speedy responses are so critical. To have any chance at candidates who are in high demand, you must be prepared to quickly assess, interview, background check, and hire. And here's the thing—just being the fastest isn't enough. Communication is essential.

Amazon Prime members receive free shipping on millions of items. They also have access to instant tracking so they know seconds after they push the "buy" button that their order has been received. Hours later, Amazon lets them know the item has been shipped and provides tracking information with the expected delivery date. The shopper is then notified once the package is delivered. Finally, Amazon sends a follow-up message to find out if the customer is happy and wishes to leave a review or order additional quantities of the product.

Your hiring funnel should include a similar tracking feature that applicants can follow with ease so they know where they stand each step of the way. If you need additional information or you want candidates to take an assessment, notify them and orient them on the process that will follow.

Try something like this: "Thanks for completing the application, Caleb. To determine if we're going to be a good fit for each other, we'd like you to take a brief online assessment that most applicants complete in 15 to 20 minutes. You can take this assessment on any Wi-Fi-enabled device at your leisure within the next 48 hours. After you complete the assessment, we will contact you by text within 24 hours with the next steps. Here's the link..."

IMPORTANT: If for any reason the applicant is disqualified and is no longer in consideration for a job with your company, do the right thing and notify them—and whenever possible, explain why this is so. Remember that every job applicant is human, and like you and me, they will feel the pain of rejection even if they weren't all the excited about the potential of working in your business. Your applicants are also customers, or potential customers, who are either going to be advocates or adversaries of your brand. So be decent, kind, and respectful, and leave them with a positive feeling about your organization.

I can't emphasize enough how important it is to communicate with candidates so they know what to expect at each stage of the recruitment process. Way too many employers leave their applicants in the dark at their own peril.

What impression of your operation do you want to leave with candidates who apply for employment at your company? Create your hiring funnel, or refine your existing one, with that objective in mind.

Tips and Tactics

Gut instinct alone isn't a reliable predictor of successful work performance or job retention. Interviews are your best tool when making strategic hiring decisions. Because there's no one right way for all employers to process applicants, the key is to create an effective hiring funnel for your business. Here are some tips:

- Train anyone who conducts interviews on how to interview properly and legally. Be aware of questions that you *cannot* legally ask, such as those that may discriminate against a candidate.

- Use hiring assessments to determine good fits for your organization. They're meant to discriminate fairly and legally, i.e., to help you separate the stand-out candidates from the lackluster or incompatible ones, NOT to target candidates for their beliefs, lifestyles, or minority status.

- Ask behavioral interview questions that can reveal how a candidate's past performance on the job or in a particular situation can predict future performance at your company.

- Use the STAR method (Situation, Task, Action, Result) to create a consistent interview process.

- Ensure interviewers understand how to rate candidates' answers to interview questions and evaluate their responses.

- Make sure your job applicants know where they stand every step of the way. Put a tracking system in place and communicate with your applicants as you would with cherished customers. Remember: The candidate experience throughout the hiring process is a vital part of building your brand as an employer of choice in your industry and community.

Chapter 17

ONBOARDING:
Your Hedge Against Turnover

Two well-intentioned parents want to give their young children a goldfish as a gift. At the pet store, the clerk places a goldfish in a plastic bag. The water in the bag is from the aquarium that the fish has been sharing for a couple of months with a number of fish friends and a few snails. Before the clerk rings them up, he asks whether the parents would like to buy a companion for the goldfish.

"It's just a fish," says Dad with a smile. "It will be fine," says Mom. They pay for the fish, along with a small fishbowl and some fish food, and head home.

At home, the parents fill the fishbowl with tap water (chlorine and all), sprinkle in some fish food, and pour the goldfish and the aquarium water from the bag into the bowl. When the kids arrive home from school, they squeal with joy upon seeing their new family member. The parents explain that Goldie, as the kids have named her, needs to be fed daily. They mention nothing about how much to feed her or how often to change her water (these details probably don't matter since it's just a fish, after all). The kids promise to feed her every single day. *Mission accomplished*, the parents think.

That evening after dinner, the kids go to visit Goldie, only to find the bowl empty. Goldie has had a severe reaction to the water in the bowl and has jumped out. She is now flopping on the table, barely alive. They hurriedly place Goldie back in the bowl. "Maybe, just maybe, we can nurse her back to health," Mom says. But as soon as they place her back in the bowl, Goldie floats lifelessly on her side.

The family next door also plans to buy a pet fish. The kids have decided to name her Ariel. But before they bring her home, they learn everything they can about how to acclimate her to their new home aquarium. Every member of the family, kids included, have done their research, and they have crafted a well-thought-out onboarding strategy. They know that with proper care, a pet goldfish can live between five and ten years. They know that proper care includes setting and following guidelines for water temperature and pH level, providing enough room for Ariel to grow in the tank, and feeding Ariel the right amount of fish food each day. They also know that when they bring her home they should turn down the lights to avoid shocking Ariel and not mix the pet store aquarium water with the tank water.

"We should also adopt one or more fish so Ariel has a friend," one of the kids says.

"That's a great idea," Dad says, "especially since research shows that fish can get lonely."

"I even read that in some countries such as Switzerland, it's against the law to keep goldfish alone," Mom says.

Before they even bring Ariel home, the family has done everything they can to ensure there will be no turnover in their aquarium. The result? Ariel arrives, thrives, and lives a long, happy life.

The Difference Between Employees Flopping and Flourishing

In both stories, the new owners' intent is to bring a goldfish home as a pet for the family to enjoy. So far, so good. But that's where the similarities end. As the two stories show, the way those goldfish are introduced into the household and treated day in and day out makes all the difference between flopping and flourishing.

The same holds true for the employees you hire. I've worked jobs where my supervisor and co-workers seemed surprised to see me on day one. Jobs where they had to scramble to find a uniform for me to wear or to figure out what paperwork I needed to complete. Jobs where I lacked the tools and equipment needed to do my job (or a desk to sit at, for that matter) because no one had thought to order them in advance.

The first day of work can be one of high expectations and great stress. New employees are introduced to the place where they'll likely spend most of their waking hours for months or, if you onboard them correctly, years to come. The onboarding experience (or lack thereof) can make or break the future of the employees you hire *and* the future of your organization.

Onboarding is the process of integrating new employees into an organization from before their first official day of work until they are successfully performing the jobs they were hired for and are fully engaged in your company and your culture. (Notice that I said it's a *process*, not an event.)

Like me, you might recall old-school onboarding "events," short orientations where you sat silently as an HR rep explained policies, procedures, and benefits and then handed over a stack of paperwork that needed to be completed. Like me, you may even remember some "fancier" onboarding events that involved a quick building tour and a formal slideshow (or the standard company video) presentation by company personnel.

News flash: Many companies are still holding one-day (or one-hour) onboarding events for their new employees (and a surprising number have no onboarding at all).

After reading this chapter, you'll make absolutely certain that your company isn't one of them.

Turnover Can Kill a Thriving Business

WARNING: You might read on and think, "Whoa! This onboarding stuff can get expensive! I need to get an ROI on my new hires as quickly as possible, and for that they've gotta be out in the field working rather than in here meeting each other, training, and learning about the company. I'll take the discounted, streamlined version of onboarding, thank you very much."

Allow me to set you straight. When done effectively, onboarding does indeed require an investment of both time and money. But when compared with the turnover costs you're suffering because you're not effectively onboarding your people, it's one of the safest and highest-yielding investments you can make in your business. There's no downside to having an effective employee onboarding process.

The average annual turnover rate across industries is more than 20 percent. That means that a business with 5 employees will lose 1 every year, and a business with 50 employees will lose 10. Now if that scares you, you had better sit down, because the turnover rate in sectors such as retail, hospitality, and food services is between 50 and 100 percent each year. Imagine having to replace half of your workforce each year—or your entire workforce each year! (Maybe you don't have to imagine it. Maybe you're living it...)

Turnover costs include what you've spent to hire, onboard, train, and develop employees. Whether you have a handful of employees or hundreds, turnover takes a huge bite out of your bottom line. Many experts estimate the cost of turnover for an entry-level worker at 30 to 50 percent of what you'd pay if they had worked for you for a full year. Losing a $12/hour employee might cost you thousands once you calculate the expense of recruiting that employee, running background checks, interviewing them, outfitting them, and training them so they're producing for you. Having them quit suddenly is painful enough. But if they suddenly quit and go to work for your competitor? That really hurts.

Now if we're talking about a skilled or mid-level position, that 30 to 50 percent turnover cost jumps to 150 to 200 percent because of the size of the investment you've made in that employee. And—hold on to your hat—losing a senior leader or executive can cost upwards of 400 percent of their annual salary!

No matter how you slice it, turnover costs are a dagger in the heart of every business owner, leader, or manager.

This age-old axiom is so true: "It's not what you make; it's what you keep." There's simply no bigger drain on your ability to "keep what you make" than losing your employees.

How Much Is Going Down Your Drain?

You can calculate your organization's turnover rate by dividing the number of employees who have left (voluntarily and involuntarily) by the average number of employees at your company. Then multiply that number by 100.

Turnover Rate = (# of Separations / Average # of Employees) x 100

Calculating the Savings of Reduced Turnover

If you want to persuade leaders in your organization to adopt a more intentional hiring process, this turnover return-on-investment calculator can provide you with bottom-line data to support your case.

Turnover ROI Calculator: https://www.shl.com/en/ customers/turnover-roi-calculator/

> # New Hires Who Say Their "First Day Was Their Worst Day" Often Sour and Disengage

Enlightened employers recognize that a primary goal of onboarding, starting with day one, is to confirm to employees that they made the right choice in working for you and to encourage them to stay for the long haul. Strategic, personalized onboarding programs can yield positive business results. For example, research by Glassdoor finds that a good onboarding program can increase new hire retention by 82 percent and productivity by more than 70 percent. These numbers are astounding.

Research by Gallup finds that employees who rate their onboarding program as exceptional are twice as likely to believe they are prepared to succeed on the job. (Interestingly enough, only 12 percent of employees say their company is great at onboarding). And when onboarding includes a professional development plan, employees are 3.5 times more likely to strongly agree that their onboarding experience was positive. A 2019 study by TalentLMS reports that most employees who have a positive onboarding experience feel valued at work, feel accepted by peers, and become more productive more quickly.

Would you want your new hire to say, "I love the company I work for!"? Would you want the new kid to tell others, "I was born to do this job! I know I'll knock it out of the park!"? Would you want your new employee to tell friends and family, "I have a future with this company! They believe in me!"?

Duh. Of course you would. That's why I'm going to show you how onboarding is an essential part of making your organization a great place to work.

Jason's First Day

Jason, an apprentice plumber, has been hired at a plumbing franchise in Scottsdale, Arizona. Here's an outline of his first day on the job.

7:45 A.M. Welcome. Jason pulls into the company parking lot, where he's warmly greeted by Reggie, a team member who has been assigned as Jason's onboarding buddy. Reggie emphasizes that he'll be a touchpoint for Jason during the first few months and beyond. A week earlier, Reggie called Jason to set clear expectations for Jason's first day of work and told him about how the company's culture sets up employees for success. Reggie had also e-mailed a first-day schedule to Jason, along with brief bios and pictures of the team members, an organizational chart, and a link to the company's onboarding portal, which includes work videos and employee testimonials.

Jason's supervisor, Olivia, meets Jason and Reggie at the building entrance. She welcomes Jason, shares her excitement about his joining the team, and answers his questions.

At my last job, I didn't even meet one on one with my manager until two weeks after I started, Jason thinks. And at that one-on-one, I was reprimanded for an error someone else made on the job. This place seems different!

8:00 A.M. Team Breakfast. Olivia and Reggie walk Jason to the breakroom. Hanging on the back wall is a large "Welcome, Jason!" sign, and 14 team members applaud as he enters the room. Over breakfast, each person tells him their name, their role at the company, and something about their lives and interests.

Samantha goes first. "Hi Jason! I'm Samantha, and I'm the manager of Extra Mile Service. I answer the phone and direct callers to the person who can best help them. I live six miles away in Tempe, and my husband and I have four kids and love to hike on the weekends."

One after the other, the team members introduce themselves. They also share their experiences working at the company and how they've felt after "saving the day" for their customers and turning those customers into raving fans.

8:30 A.M. Cubicle Assignment. Reggie shows Jason his locker and his cubicle. At his cubicle, Jason finds a handwritten welcome note from the company president and a welcome basket. The basket includes company swag (a shirt, hat, pens and pads, healthy snacks, and a company-branded onesie for his baby girl). The supplies Jason will need are all there, along with a list of contact information for key personnel. Reggie leaves Jason to settle in.

9:00 A.M. HR Orientation. Jason sits down with Rhonda from HR, who takes the time to learn more about Jason and his family. Rhonda explains some of the forms and paperwork that are necessary to get Jason covered on the company's insurance plan and make sure he's paid promptly. Rhonda spends most of their time together talking about the company benefits, including the bonus structure. She says that the company welcomes Jason's ideas no matter how crazy they may seem. For example, based on one employee suggestion, the company adopted new technology to route customer service calls. Based on another employee suggestion, the company now pays for employees' gym memberships.

10:00 A.M.–noon. Tour. Reggie takes Jason on a facility tour. They cover the office, the tool warehouse, and the private outdoor lot where the company vans are meticulously maintained. In each department, Jason is greeted by folks who welcome him to the company.

Along the way, Reggie stops in front of a wall that shows the company's five-year vision and roadmap. Reggie lets Jason study the display, which features pictures of employees and lists many of their personal and professional goals. Jason smiles as he sees that his picture is already hanging on the wall. *I made the right choice*, he thinks. *I belong here.*

1:00 P.M. Career Path. After lunch with Reggie, Jason's next stop is with Monique, vice president of career development. Monique administered the skills and personality assessment Jason took during the interview process, and she uses the assessment results as a starting point for a conversation about Jason's strengths and professional goals. She explains that there are four phases of a career with the company: apprentice, plumber, team lead, and supervisor. Each phase has a set of skills to master, after which time the employee is eligible for a pay raise. She also introduces a well-developed training program that includes on-the-job coaching, classroom instruction, and online modules. Monique helps Jason start building a personalized development program and leaves him to try out some of the online modules.

2:00 p.m. Ride-Along. Jason accompanies Reggie on two customer calls. The experience includes time for Jason to discuss what he has learned so far on his first day and for Reggie to answer questions.

4:30 p.m. Recap and Reflection. Jason meets with Olivia in her office. She asks about his first-day experience and gives him her full attention as she actively listens to what he has to say. *My last boss usually read e-mails on his computer or checked his phone while we met,* Jason thinks. *Because he was always multitasking, I never felt heard. This really is different!*

Olivia lays out a 90-day onboarding plan that she has customized for Jason. She asks for his input and invites him to share ideas on how the first day could have been a better experience. As they shake hands, Olivia presents Jason with a gift card for a local restaurant. "Please take your wife to dinner and welcome her to our family," she says.

5:00 p.m. Day One Is Done. Reggie escorts Jason to his car. Jason can't wait to get home to tell his wife that he has the perfect job at the best company on the planet. He also can't wait to see his baby in her little onesie sporting the company logo.

Staging and Guiding the Onboarding Process

How long should onboarding last? Experts report that it can take at least 90 days for employees to feel dialed in to a new job, confident that they can perform effectively, trusting of their manager and colleagues, and secure in their knowledge of where to go when they encounter a problem. For more complex jobs, this process can take up to a year.

Phillip Cohen, CEO of Cohen Architectural Woodworking in St. James, Missouri, brings his new employees back into the office after they complete a couple weeks on the job for an additional orientation lasting up to four hours. Then, after their first month, Phillip invites the new hires to sit down and enjoy a meal with him and his team. To prepare for this meeting with their boss, these workers are instructed to bring with them answers to several questions, like, "Now that you've been with us for a month, why do you want to continue to work here?" "Being close to home" is not a good enough answer for Phillip. He says that he wants his people to have a much deeper connection to their work than geography.

Another question they must be able to answer is "What are you doing to improve your character?" Phillip says that if his employees aren't actively working on building their character, this is not going to be a good fit for them.

Cohen's onboarding process continues for 90 days, as they are committed to building not just the highest-quality wood products, but also high-quality people who are committed to continual improvement at work and at home.

If the end game is retaining employees who are on fire at work, it makes sense that the onboarding process would take at least three months. However, 25 percent of companies onboard in one day or less, 26 percent onboard over the course of one week, and 21 percent onboard in over the course of one month. Only 11 percent of companies invest three months or more into onboarding.

To build an onboarding process with intention, you may want to put a cross-functional team in place to determine what the process should look like and who should be involved. For starters, assign team members to research ideas for onboarding and talk to peers at other companies. What are those other companies doing? What do their three-month (or three-week or three-day) onboarding processes look like? Also be sure to ask other employees about their ideas and experiences (at the company and elsewhere—learn everything possible about the good, the bad, and the truly unfortunate).

Once this team has a foundation for the onboarding practices that your organization should implement, they might anticipate and make sure their onboarders can answer the kinds of questions new hires will ask, such as the following:

- What exactly is expected of me in my new role?

- Who will I report to and work with?

- What are the tools and materials I need to do my job?

- Who do I contact if I have a problem?

- Why is my job important? How can I excel at this company?

- What is my future with the company?

Next, this team might compile questions that the organization could answer to ensure onboarding is as effective as possible. I've included some examples below.

- What are some qualitative and quantitative outcomes from the onboarding process?

  These outcomes can be for the new employee, the team (if applicable), the company, and/or the customers. Examples include engagement levels, feedback from managers on new hire performance, retention data after 90 days and one year, feedback on employees serving as company champions, and new hire clarity about role and expectations.

- How long will the onboarding process last? What are the steps and stages of onboarding?

- What specific things will we do to help new hires learn our company's culture starting on day one?

- Who will be involved in developing and refining onboarding processes (e.g., supervisor, team members, HR), and what will their roles and responsibilities be?

- What personnel and financial resources will we need to develop and implement the onboarding plan?

Onboarding Best Practices

Pre-boarding—assign an onboarding buddy before your new hire starts. You can take a number of actions before an employee starts to make that employee feel welcome and valued and to help introduce them to your culture. One valuable pre-boarding step is to partner the new employee with an onboarding buddy. According to the Human Capital Institute, almost 90 percent of organizations that pair a new hire with a buddy during the onboarding process find that it's an effective strategy to help the new worker become more productive sooner.

The buddy should be a friendly, gregarious, engaged employee who is at the same level as (or slightly above) someone who has performed well in the role that the new employee is undertaking. And it should be someone who willingly volunteers for the role. The buddy should exchange contact information with the new employee, as a number of questions are sure to arise when the new employee is away from work. The buddy should be in touch with the employee after the formal hiring and before the employee's first day to make sure the employee knows all about the logistics of the first day—where to park, what to wear, and what security procedures to follow (if applicable).

In addition, the buddy can do the following:

- Make sure the new employee has access to paperwork to review or complete before the first day of work, as well as provide access to important information about the company.

- Reinforce a realistic job preview, answer any questions, and listen to any concerns.

- Greet the employee at the front door or in the parking lot on day one and walk the employee to the location where onboarding will begin.

- Show the employee around, introduce them to their colleagues, and show them where they can find available resources.

- Check in regularly (once or twice a week) throughout the onboarding process to find out what the employee likes about the job and the company, what has been the greatest thrill so far, what concerns the employee has, and what ideas the employee has for improvement.

The first day. Structure a planned, personalized series of experiences. Yes, you may want to set aside time for paperwork that hasn't been completed beforehand, but the emphasis should be on establishing connections with other team members and helping the employee understand the company culture. One key connection will be with their direct supervisor, who can communicate clear expectations for the job and the onboarding process.

The first week. Blend initial training and development with more in-depth meetings with team members across departments. Employees should be encouraged to include the new hire in breaks, meals, and other opportunities for social interaction. The buddy and the supervisor should check in to make sure the new hire is beginning to feel comfortable and building confidence.

The first month. Continue building experiences, knowledge, and confidence. Involve the employee in meetings, scheduling, and planning.

Recognize that the first 30 days may be a time to reinforce the basics, building a foundation that can lead to job competence and mastery. Remember: People have different learning styles and build skills at their own pace, which may be faster or slower than you expect. Be prepared to adapt the learning plan accordingly.

Months two and three. Do not assume that the employee is fully integrated. The supervisor should observe performance on the job and provide constructive and timely feedback. It should start to be clear whether the employee would like more autonomy or may need more structure in terms of coaching and management. Their buddy should continue to check in. The buddy, supervisor, and other relevant personnel may also want to compare perspectives regarding the information, guidance, and feedback they're providing to the new candidate, as well as compare feedback that the employee has provided.

Months four through six. Continue training, team-building, and measuring performance; continue regular check-ins; celebrate milestones and successes; and make plans for what happens beyond the six-month mark.

Successful Transition

Properly implemented, the onboarding process should enable candidates to master their jobs and reinforce their long-term commitment and transition to the company.

Here are five indicators of a successful transition:[9]

I.   **Social cohesion.** New employees fit in (they're not a fish out of water), they feel respected and valued, and they feel that they're part of a team.

---

9   Adapted from research conducted by Helena D. Cooper-Thomas, a New Zealand-based organizational behavior academic, and Neil Anderson, a professor in HR management at the University of Amsterdam.

2. **Effective performance.** New employees are performing successfully in the roles for which they were hired.

3. **Extra-mile performance.** New employees show on-fire engagement, going above and beyond to help out, fill in, and offer ideas to improve effectiveness and efficiency at work.

4. **Retention.** New employees feel at home as part of the family and will stick around rather than look for the quickest exit.

5. **Reinforcement of your culture and your brand.** New hires tell friends and family about their great experience at work. Another tipping point is when they start saying "we" instead of "they" when talking about the people with whom they work.

Tips and Tactics

With the average turnover rate across industries exceeding 20 percent and some industries experiencing more than 50 percent turnover annually, the impact of employee turnover on your bottom line is immense. A solid onboarding program can help. Here are some tips to follow when building your program:

- Recognize the value of effective onboarding in terms of developing and retaining employees. Most importantly, make your onboarding process a real, ongoing process rather than a one-day or one-week "event."

- Convene a team to design an onboarding process that will work for your company. Review the best practice ideas in this chapter and invite recommendations from others at the company. In addition, consider if you would like to customize onboarding with various segments of your employee population, such as veterans, older hires, and temp employees.

- Determine specific ways to help your new employee understand your company culture right out of the gate. It's this culture and the ways in which each and every employee lives that culture every day that will keep your employee invested in their job and the success of your company.

- Document your onboarding process so it's standard for each new hire, and update that process as you make changes. Your goals are to make sure your business is a great place to work and to help acclimate new employees to your business environment so they recognize and value the opportunity to work for you. What worked two years ago may not work now, so evolve your onboarding process over time.

- Assign an onboarding buddy to your new hires before they start. The buddy will help new hires feel welcome and connected to the company from day one.

- Determine how you will measure the success of your onboarding process—for the employee, the teams they support, the company, and your customers.

Chapter 18

THE ONLY REAL RETENTION STRATEGY

There is no Santa Clause. There is no Spiderman. No Big Foot. And no such thing as the Tooth Fairy.

And it's taken me years of in-depth research with hundreds of companies and thousands of managers to realize that there is no such thing as an effective strategy for retaining an employee who wants to leave you for a similar job with a similar company in the same geographical area.

Look, if one of your people has a valid reason for quitting their job (e.g., a geographic move, retirement, an illness, a pressing family matter, a significant career change, etc.) there's not a lot that you—or any other employer—can do to keep them.

Every time you find yourself in danger of losing a valued employee to another employer that wants them in a similar role, you stand at the precipice of a negotiation. This is the point where, in order to get them to change their mind, you must now offer that employee a promotion, a higher salary, more vacation/paid time off, permission to work from home, or a combination of any number of perks and working conditions. But even if you are successful in your negotiation and convince the employee to stay, you haven't discovered some secret retention tactic. All you've done is transferred some of the chips from your pile to their pile. Consider it a temporary remedy that will last until the next time they force you back to the negotiation table.

If you're searching for a *real* employee retention strategy, I know of only one:

If you hire the right people (not the *best* people, but the *right* people—those who are ideally suited for your culture and who possess the technical skills and the talents required to handle the job, as well as the work ethic you demand) and you treat them better than another employer promises to treat them for performing in a similar role, you won't need a retention strategy because your people aren't going to leave.

Why would they?

So let's go back to the very premise of this book and agree that America—and for that matter, most of the industrialized world—is smack dab in the middle of the tightest labor market in 50 years.

And because not only are ordinary workers in high demand and short supply, but also *skilled* workers who possess a solid *work ethic* are in even higher demand and shorter supply, this is, unarguably, the worst labor market EVER.

I hope we can also agree that in order to find and keep great people in your business, you have to be better than the competition (i.e., any company that wants the same people you do) on two fronts:

I. You have to be a better place to work than they are.

2. You have to be a more creative and more relentless recruiter than they are.

If you're not 100 percent willing and committed to do both 1 & 2 above, perhaps it's because you're patiently waiting for a new crop of job-ready candidates armed with the work ethic you demand to graduate from high school or college and knock on your door. Unfortunately, that's not going to happen anytime soon. But still, some employers today are sitting around their metaphorical fireplace waiting for their perfect-fit employees to drop down the chimney.

My experience has shown me that today's employers can be divided into one of two camps. Some are whining and moaning about the shallow labor pool and the higher wages they are being forced to pay. They're waiting for something to change "out there" that will solve their labor problems. In the other camp are those who are consistently evolving to put themselves in a position to find and keep the best available workers. The employers in this camp begin each day by asking themselves three questions:

1. How can we be the best company to work for in this industry and/or this community?

2. How can we improve our recruiting efforts across all of the various talent pools where potential great hires might be available to us (e.g., employee referrals, schools and colleges, ex-offenders, returning military, etc.)?

3. To achieve our goal of being FULLY STAFFED with the right people, what is it that we can do to find and keep the people that we need that our competitors are unwilling and/or unprepared to do?

It doesn't take a genius to show you that if you're not in the camp with the employers asking these three questions, you're in the first camp by default.

Even if you have unsexy jobs that you think nobody wants, the truth is that there are some good fits (a.k.a. Bradys) out there that can be had. If you're determined to expand your search and not leave any stone unturned and you're open to changing your recruiting tactics, you can hire and retain them in your business. But if you're of a mindset that the good old days are history and that there aren't any good people out there anymore who really want to work, you might as well throw this book in the dumpster and keep fishing for anyone you can find with a "Help Wanted" sign and an ad on Craigslist. Just know that it's going to take a lot more than a recession to repair the gaping hole in your labor pool.

There is no magic formula, no silver bullet solution, and no quick fix to remedy your labor woes. If you're going to start winning the battle for talent in your business, brace yourself for a marathon, not a 100-yard dash. Stop searching for a retention secret and roll up your shirt sleeves to work on improving all facets of your hiring process as you simultaneously strive to better your workplace culture.

Cut to the Chase

Imagine you and I are seated on a flight that's landing in 25 minutes. The overhead announcement instructs us to turn off and stow our electronics, and we suddenly find ourselves in a conversation asking each other about our work. You tell me that you run a small business and are having a horrible time hanging on to employees, especially those you rely on to perform hard, "unsexy" jobs. I respond that I am a workforce researcher and have just completed a book that provides proven answers on that exact topic. You then grab my arm and say, "Look, we're going to be going our own separate ways in a few minutes. I'm not a big reader, so can you please cut to the chase and help me crack the code on how I can keep good people in my organization?"

Without blinking, I would share the following five things that would significantly reduce turnover in your organization:

1. Make "employees first" your credo. There's always a mention of how a company feels about their employees inscribed in their corporate mission statement and their core values.

"We love our people."

"Our people are our biggest asset."

"Our people are our strength."

"Yeah, right," the cynic dwelling inside me scoffs. Then why is it that so very few of the frontline employees I've interviewed over the past 20 years (and those interviews number in the thousands) actually know their employer's mission statement and core values? And for the frontliners who have memorized those lofty platitudes (by company mandate), why do so many of them roll their eyes with disdain as they sarcastically recite them?

The truth is that your underlying promise to employees has got to be more than a great-sounding slogan handsomely framed on your boardroom wall and slapped on your company's online hiring portal. Your commitment to your people needs to be the driving force behind your market proposition and an integral part of your competitive strategy. The demonstrated follow-through on this commitment to your employees has to be an agenda item at every leadership meeting you have, and the decisions that result have to be felt by all those who are manning your front lines. Then, and only then, are employees your priority.

2. Discover *their* story. The overwhelming majority of employers I've studied spend the vast majority of time informing. They want to make certain that employees know the history of the company, their own personal history of how they came to work for the company, how and why the company is successful, and what sets them apart from the competitors, and as many policies, rules, and regulations as they can dump into the brains of their new hires. Conversely, the leaders and managers that engage their new hires from day one do the complete opposite. The primary focus is learning about the employee.

Great leaders don't just tell their story; they invest time into getting to know the story of their people, and they seek to find common ground on which the can form a deeper relationship with them. They want to know their people's strengths, goals, and dreams. They discover what their people are passionate about when they are not at work, and they figure out exactly what inspires them to bring their very best effort to the job every day. And as we learned from MAACO's Brian Greenley, knowing the stories of your people is essential for building long-term loyalty.

3. Flex 'til it hurts. The current workforce includes multiple generations that are characterized by different experiences, motivations, plans, and patterns. In other words, employees are individuals. It no longer makes sense to promote a one-size-fits-all workplace where everyone is forced to conform to *all* the same policies and stringent rules. Instead, make your workplace a place where everybody is treated fairly and held to the same high standards of quality, service, and integrity, but also one that can conform to the special needs of your people under varying circumstances.

David Stein, an area developer and franchisee of Office Pride Commercial Cleaning Services in Tyler, Texas, puts it this way: "Our workers come from a wide array of backgrounds. So rather than being transactional, we aim to be transformational. We know that many of our employees have another job or perhaps even two jobs. I want those people and I go out of my way to hire them because they've already shown that they have the discipline to hold a job. So if a guy tells me he can work 10 hours a week—he gets 10 hours, no more, no less. If a woman tells me she's got a big family to take care of and can only work 6 hours on Saturdays, I say "GREAT! You're hired!"

Titan Restoration in Mesa, Arizona, started with 5 people in 2005 and now has over 50. The company offers employees unlimited paid vacation. Says owner Russ Palmer: "We think that work-life balance and a time to decompress and spend with people you care about is important to retention." Palmer further explains: "We focus on performance. And if an employee is performing based on our goals and standards, taking 25–30 days a year paid vacation makes good business sense for us. There are some caveats: Except for emergencies, employees are expected to give advance notice. They also are expected to ensure their job duties are completed or covered." Even though it's not every young child's dream to someday work in a job where they clean up after a fire or a torrential storm and remediate mold or remove biohazardous contaminants, this "unlimited paid vacation" perk is obviously enough to find and keep some really talented people.

4. Help 'em grow...and then let 'em go. I know this sounds counterintuitive. After all, why would you train an employee to the point that they'd outgrow the opportunities your business can provide for their advancement? For two reasons, actually:

- Their increased skill level will pay dividends for as long as they remain in your business.

- Any employee worth a darn is going to leave you when they stop learning and growing.

Training leads to longevity more than it results in turnover. Employees value opportunities for personal development and growth often as much as they do a salary increase. Research shows that if you invest in developing your people, they are less likely to get bored and grow stagnant, and they are more likely to stay with you, because they feel enlightened, inspired, and challenged.

No matter what business you're in, your employees aren't going to be the same tomorrow as they are today. They're either going to get better, or they're going to get worse. The difference between those two extremes is you. And if you're not growing your people, their productivity and performance are going to erode, and eventually, they'll be stuck in neutral and no other employer is even going to want them.

But do you really want an employee whose skills are diminishing or are no longer relevant and they're not wanted anywhere else?

It's essential to have a growth and development plan for each and every employee, one that they have had a voice in creating and that they are excited about. And if this results in so much growth that you can't do justice to their career, don't just *let* them go; *encourage* them to go, and do everything in your power to help them find and secure a better job.

Brady dreams of designing hydroelectrical systems for a leading manufacturer. You can bet I'm going to work every contact I have in my database—and leverage the contacts that the colleagues in my network will share—to make sure Brady lands an amazing job upon graduation. Lord knows he deserves that. And on the flip side, I deserve a Brady clone, and I am 100 percent certain that when word of Brady's experience at Camelot Car and Dog Wash spreads through the halls of the mechanical engineering building at the Colorado School of Mines, his replacement will be fired up and eager to scoop some mud and install a few solenoids.

5. Crank up the FQ (fun quotient). The pressure to innovate, produce more, and perform at a higher level consistently has never been greater. It's not only the worst labor market ever; it's also the most competitive economic climate ever. I don't need to prove this with some sort of study or statistic. You know it's true. The stress and anxiety you feel is real, and it's being passed on to everyone in your organization. The result? A sometimes-tense work environment that can affect your employees' job satisfaction as well as their productivity.

So isn't it about time you wore one of those cheap red clown noses to work or purposely sat on a whoopy cushion at your next meeting? Your employees might think you'd totally lost it, but at least they'd have a giggle. And that would take the stress meter down a notch in the precise direction it needs to go.

No, you don't have to put a ping pong table in your warehouse. But if there's space, it might be a good idea. Actually, anything you can do to get your people smiling, laughing, or even talking about something other than work and their personal problems is a very good idea. Form a Wednesday afternoon bowling league. Hire a local rock band to perform at your Monday morning meeting. Take your people to a ball game, or skydiving, or to the zoo. Regardless of what you choose, decide to do something that will ignite some laughter and lighten the burden.

And then do something even more unexpected next month or next week. Just get the ball rolling, and once people can see that it's not just a one-time gimmick, get out of the way and let your people keep things rolling. Sure, you'll need some boundaries, but don't worry about those now. I can assure you that if you strive to make your workplace a happier, more fun place for your employees, turnover will drop like you wouldn't believe.

Go Bananas and Win the Recruiting and Retention War

Is it possible to create a workplace culture that is so unique and dynamic that it could literally shake the foundation of "America's favorite pastime" to its core? Jesse Cole not only believes this possible; he's actively doing just that.

Jesse and his wife, Emily, are founders and owners of the Savannah Bananas, a college summer league baseball team that replaced the city's minor league team that left due to poor fan support. The Coles had to sell their home to purchase an expansion franchise in 2015, but they could manage to sell only one season ticket the first couple of months they were in business.

Over the next off-season, they created a Fans First culture that places their employees as the most important Fans in the operation, and BAM!—the Savannah Bananas now sell out a 4,000-plus-seat stadium every single game and have for the past three years. A miraculous turnaround by any measure.

Going to a Savannah Bananas baseball game is not just "something to do" on a warm summer evening; it has become THE thing to do in this vibrant coastal city of Georgia. I know this firsthand because my wife and I flew from Denver to Savannah while researching this book just to attend one of those games (…err, should I say, experience one of those events) to see if all the hype surrounding this burgeoning enterprise is truly merited.

Man oh man, is it!

It's difficult for me to capture in words the energy, passion, drive, and imagination that is behind the Bananas phenomenon. When Lori and I arrived at the stadium two hours before the first pitch, there was already a long line of fans waiting to get in. These fans weren't bored. In fact, they were being royally entertained by a 20-piece band, a crazy DJ zig-zagging through the crowd on a Segway, a six-year-old giving high

From Left, Head Coach Tyler Gillum, Eric, and Bananas Owner, Jessie Cole.

fives, and the team's mascot taking selfies with the fans and handing out free Savannah Bananas team swag.

And right out front, shaking hands and welcoming each guest was Jesse Cole, dressed from head to toe in his signature yellow tux with a tall yellow top hat. Determined to make this 95-year-old stadium appear brand new, Jesse walked from end to end, picking up any trash that may have been passed over by the stadium's grounds crew, our first indication that that Bananas are led by a do-as-I-do CEO.

Jesse Cole impresses you as a cross between P.T. Barnum and Walt Disney. He's insanely creative, incredibly positive, and joyfully enthusiastic about every aspect of his people and his business. The Savannah Bananas' revenues are outperforming all other teams in this league in a significant, if not embarrassing, way. The concession sales alone from the Savannah Bananas exceed the total revenues from several other teams in his league.

The players perform hip hop moves between innings. The wonderful cheerleaders are not 18-year-old models-in-waiting, but 65-year-old retirees. The first base coach is a break-dancing fool. And every ticket to every game comes with free all-you-can-eat hot dogs, burgers, chicken sandwiches, chips, popcorn, water, soda, and cookies. *When was the last time you attended **any** game, movie, concert, or attraction where the food and drink were included in the price of your ticket?*

I'm just scratching the surface and could go on and on. But suffice it to say, an evening at a Savannah Bananas game is remarkably and refreshingly different from anything I've ever seen.

As I marveled at what Lori and I were experiencing, I asked Jesse to share the number one secret to his success. Without pausing he began to gush about his employees. And he insisted I meet his people, from VPs in the front office to the ushers in the bleachers.

Jesse and Emily's *Fans First Playbook* is the closest thing to what you might call an employee handbook. Instead of citing a lot of rules and procedures, this colorful guide outlines the ins and outs of the fascinating Savannah Bananas culture. Check out a few of the "policies":

Vacations? *Take one whenever you'd like.*

Dress code? *That's your call. (Although we consider you a critical cast member in front of the fans, so your appearance does matter.)*

Working hours? *Except for on game days, you choose them. Just make sure your work is done well and on schedule.*

Wages? *You name your own salary.* (Hard to believe, right? Read on.)

That's not to say there aren't very high expectations for employees. This playbook has simply been designed as "a resource for you in support of your growth."

Jesse's leadership principle is simple and profound:

- "Love your customers more than you love your product."
- "Love your employees more than you love your customers."

And it's evident that he and Emily are living this out with every move they make. Inside the *Playbook*, you'll see sections like:

Always and Never:

Always	Never
Be on stage	Break character
Take ownership	Makes excuses
Find a solution	Say "no"
Ask questions	Assume
Beat the greet	Wait for "hello"
Recognize kids	Only address adults
Say "thank you" when guests exit	Leave before fans

Be Your Superhero

"Everyone plays a role in our cast. Together we deliver the Fans First Show. Every detail matters. Your clothes. Your hair. Your makeup. Your facial expression. Your voice. Your tone. Your greeting. What is your superhero version of yourself? How could you amplify that to be the best version of yourself to the fans?"

Everyone Is a Janitor

This philosophy is one that Jesse adapted from Disney, a company he greatly admires. At Grayson Stadium, every single employee from Jesse to the clarinet player in the band has the responsibility for keeping everything—from the parking lot to the restrooms—clean and orderly. If an employee sees a piece of trash, without giving it a second thought, they are to pick it up and dispose of it properly. If the napkin dispenser at the concession stand is running low, they are taught to refill it. It doesn't matter if you're one of his executives, the bass drum player, or the team's short stop. He says, "We are all the Savannah Bananas, and this is *our* castle!" (This explains why we saw Jesse scurrying about the stadium before the game picking up all the trash he noticed.)

Recruiting and Interviews—They Are Hunters

Jesse and his team leverage the power of video and social media as a means to hunt great prospects. That's why it's easy to find a number of videos on YouTube, Facebook, etc., showing exactly what it's like to work for the Savannah Bananas. But the videos don't glamorize the unsexy parts of working for the Bananas. The messaging is clear to let prospective applicants know "you're not a good fit if you can't handle change, or working 4p to 11p shifts three times each week." They even produced a video to show what type of people should NOT apply for a job.

To be transparent, part-time job applicants are warned in advance that if money is their primary motivator, this is not going to be their "pot of gold" opportunity. "This can be a part of your income, but not the main part," they inform job seekers. "Your paycheck is not going to best thing you're going to get from your job."

The Bananas application process involves submitting a traditional résumé as well as a video cover letter that details:

- your future résumé (where are you planning to be and what are you planning to do in five, ten, and fifteen years?)

- and a short description of how you embrace and live out the six qualities of their Fans First Way philosophy: *"Always Be Caring, Different, Enthusiastic, Fun, Growing, and Hungry."*

Onboarding

After they are hired, the new employee is immersed in an onboarding process that makes them feel as welcome as if they were brought in as a first-round draft pick. Every employee's first day is celebrated and acknowledged on LinkedIn. They are celebrated upon arrival with silly string, their favorite meal and favorite snacks (which have been determined in their job interview), pictures on their desk, and their photo proudly displayed on the wall along with Jesse's, Emily's, and the rest of the leaders'. The new hires receive a copy of the *Fans First Playbook*, setting expectations for their performance and serving as their personal road map for growth and success.

Retention? "It's our culture, not a strategy"

Jesse believes that if you empower your employees (allowing them to pick their schedule, have significant input on their compensation, etc.), retention will cease to be an issue; thus, no strategy for keeping them is needed. "If you have proactive conversations with employees and you have a sense of what they want for the future (e.g., future resume/roadmap) and help them get there, they'll be much less likely to turnover because they had a bad day or can get $1 more per hour somewhere else," Jesse told me. "We take FUN seriously, but we never take ourselves too seriously. If we're not having fun, we can't deliver fun to our fans."

Employees Naming Their Own Salaries? That's Crazy! (So Crazy, It Works)

Professionalism is boring. Weird wins.
—Savannah Bananas *Fans First Playbook*

After a great season, Jesse wanted to raise salaries across the board for all employees but wasn't quite sure of how much each person deserved. So rather than guess and conjure up some arbitrary amount, he approached his entire staff and asked them to put a number down for what their next salary would be. As soon as he did it, he got queasy and felt like he might have just made a big mistake. "What in the world were we thinking?" Jesse thought. "Most of our people wrote down serious raises of up to 30 percent. But we asked them, so we held our ground and said 'yes' to every single request."

And what was the impact of that *crazy* decision? "Since giving those raises, business is up almost 150 percent. In fact, our revenue over that period eclipses what every other team in our league will do this entire year. I truly believe that if you trust and empower your people and really take great care of them, amazing things will come back your way." Now Bananas employees are participating in profit sharing, and their performance continues to climb.

I closed this chapter and this book with the story about Jesse and the Savannah Bananas to cement my fundamental point. No matter what business or industry you're in, no matter how barren the labor landscape appears from your office window, there are, indeed, great fits for your organization hiding in plain sight. But they're not going to come to you without any effort or creativity on your part. And even then, they still won't sign on—and stay on—unless you've got one thing firmly established: an amazing workplace culture. In today's tough labor market, the job hunters have become the hunted, and it's the employers' responsibility to target and secure their prime "catches."

From utilizing thoughtful, unique, and digitally-minded job advertising techniques; to leveraging the power of community, educational, and governmental networks and programs; to harnessing the value in under-tapped labor pools like veterans, retirees, ex-offenders, and people with disabilities; to optimizing your onboarding and retention processes, it takes a host of modern staffing strategies to get an edge over your competitors and find and keep the best fits for your open and future positions.

If you commit the same energy and resources into recruiting great people as you put into attracting new customers and you form the habit of relentlessly evaluating and improving every facet of your workplace culture, you will come to the place where you can proudly say,

"My business is FULLY STAFFED!"

INDEX

A

D

E

G

H

K

L

N

O

P

Q

R

T

Two Maids and a Mop, 59

X

Y

Z

ABOUT THE AUTHOR

Since 1998, Eric Chester has been the leading voice in recruiting, training, managing, motivating, and retaining the emerging workforce.

As an in-the-trenches workplace researcher and renowned employee engagement expert, Chester knows what it takes to attract today's enigmatic talent and get them to perform at their best. *Fully Staffed* is his sixth leadership book. His two most recent releases, *On Fire at Work – How Great Companies Ignite Passion in Their People Without Burning Them Out* (2015) and *Reviving Work Ethic – A Leader's Guide to Ending Entitlement and Restoring Pride in the Workforce* (2012), have been widely acclaimed by employers all over the world.

Eric Chester is a Hall of Fame Keynote Speaker who has delivered more than 2,300 paid speeches on three continents. His clients include Harley Davidson, McDonald's, AT&T, The US Army, and Allstate, to name a few.

EricChester.com

303-239-9999